TRUMPING TRUDEAU

HOW DONALD TRUMP WILL CHANGE CANADA
EVEN IF JUSTIN TRUDEAU DOESN'T KNOW IT YET

EZRA LEVANT

Printed in Canada

First Printing, 2017

ISBN-13: 978-1542526203
ISBN-10: 1542526205

Rebel News Network Ltd.
PO Box 73536, Wychwood PO
Toronto, ON M6C4A7

Front cover photo credit: Gage Skidmore

Cover and book design by Saundra Jones, Torch Agency.

CONTENTS

TRUMPING TRUDEAU

INTRODUCTION

THE ERA OF TRUDEAU IS OVER

The Justin Trudeau Era lasted precisely 386 days.

It began on October 19, 2015 — when Trudeau was elected Prime Minister of Canada.

Back then, everything seemed possible. Trudeau would usher in a new liberal era, in perfect harmony with like-minded liberals in the White House.

It was going to last forever. Trudeau was just 43 years old. His own father, Pierre Trudeau, had served as Prime Minister for sixteen years. Why couldn't junior, too?

The media was certain of it. Sure, Trudeau won just 39% of the popular vote — hardly a landslide. But that 39% included all the people who mattered — social justice warriors, environmental activists, Muslim students societies, minor celebrities and major lobbyists. Canada's journalism union even registered as a third-party Elections Canada "SuperPAC" to formally campaign for Trudeau.

It wasn't just that Trudeau was liberal. It was the promise of a dynasty — the return of Pierre Trudeau's style, and maybe with it, the leftist policies of the 1960s and '70s. No more fussy economists like Stephen Harper and the Conservatives saying "no" all the time. Here was Mr. Yes, who would tax and spend and regulate and decree so hard, he'd undo the Harper decade of restraint. But more important than just boring money talk, Trudeau would ensure that "Canada is back!" — back to holding fashionable opinions at the United Nations, back to triangulating against the United States, back to jet-setting through the Third World and playing an "honest broker" between Israel and terrorist groups.

Trudeau was happy to play Robin to Barack Obama's Batman — two selfie-posing cool kids who really "got it." And Trudeau was eager to be a mini-me to Hillary Clinton, too. It would be just more proof of Trudeau's feminist credentials. It was going to be amazing. Trudeau and Clinton even shared campaign advisors.

And then, on November 8, 2016, Donald Trump happened. That ended Clinton's dreams. But it also marked the end of the Trudeau moment, almost before it even began.

November 8 was a shocking night — for the pundits, pollsters and for Clinton herself, who had been so sure of victory, she simply could not bring herself to appear in public until the next morning.

But Justin Trudeau? He's still in denial. Actually, he's still in campaign mode — still chirping snide little remarks about Trump to the media; still tweaking America's nose in passive-aggressive stunts; still rooting for his defeated Democrat friends, instead of preparing for a working relationship with the 45th president of the United States.

Donald Trump has been busy choosing his cabinet and engaging with the countries that have always captured his attention — like China, Mexico and Israel. When he inevitably turns his gaze to Canada, our country will get the full Trump treatment. But what will that be?

A lot of that is up to Trudeau and his advisors. When Obama succeeded George W. Bush, Stephen Harper was faced with a counterpart who couldn't have been more different — both ideologically and stylistically. But Harper was a grown-up about it — he even replaced Canada's ambassador to the U.S. with a gregarious former NDP premier, Gary Doer, to better match the new temperament in Washington, D.C.

What will Trudeau do? Will he seek to align his economic policies with Trump's — tax cuts and a renaissance of fossil fuels? Will he support Trump's new foreign policy approach, based on national sovereignty and national interests?

Or will Trudeau position himself as the world's leader of the opposition to Trump — the role Pierre Trudeau took so often during the Cold War — by rhetorically undermining the U.S. and defining Canada as his father so often did: as the un-America?

Trumping Trudeau shows just how totally Trump's victory changes everything in Canada — and is a warning to those who would seek to turn Canada into road-kill, in the face of Trump's political juggernaut.

ONE

JUSTIN TRUDEAU
HATES DONALD TRUMP

Justin Trudeau hates Donald Trump.

Trudeau's whole team does — his MPs, his cabinet ministers, his campaign staff. They know they shouldn't say so publicly, but they just can't help themselves.

To be fair, many Canadian politicians — even some Conservative politicians — disparaged Trump as he fought his way to the top of the Republican Party, and then through the most brutal presidential election campaign in memory. All the critics thought disparaging Trump was an easy way to score points — taking pot-shots at a man everyone agreed had no chance of winning.

But Trudeau turned Trump-bashing into an art form. His Liberal Party even used Trump as fodder for fundraising campaigns, right until the end.

In late September 2016 — just six weeks before the U.S. election — the Liberals sent out a massive e-mail blast to party supporters, demonizing Trump and praising Hillary Clinton. The subject of the Liberal e-mail was, rather bizarrely, the presidential debate in the U.S. But the letter was much more than a partisan endorsement of Clinton. It was a demonization of Trump, an attempt to turn his very name into an insult to blacken Trudeau's political opponents at home. "Hope or fear? Diversity or division? Openness and inclusion, or turning our backs on the world?" read the fundraising letter. "This kind of negative, divisive politics builds walls between Canadians — and it shows us all how much is at stake." It was one of several Trump-bashing e-mails Trudeau sent out — so it must have been a financial success.

Trudeau didn't hide his contempt in under-the-radar fundraising e-mails to the party faithful. He made a campaign-style visit in New York City — at the United Nations, right across the street from Trump World Tower — to bash Trump's campaign platform in his own home town.

Trudeau didn't mention Trump by name at that UN speech on September 20, but his spin doctors made sure every sleepy journalist knew who he was talking about. It was Trudeau returning the favour for Hillary Clinton, whose campaign staff had been an integral part of his own election just one year before.

"When leaders are faced with citizens' anxiety, we have a choice to make. Do we exploit that anxiety or do we allay it?" asked Trudeau. "Exploiting it is easy."

Trudeau took special aim at Trump's plans for increased vetting of Muslim immigrants. "Because what is the alternative? To exploit anxiety? To turn it into fear and blame? To reject others because they look, or speak, or pray differently than we do? You see, in Canada we got a very important thing right. Not perfect, but right. In Canada, we see diversity as a source of strength, not weakness."

Perhaps Trudeau was channeling his mentor, former Prime Minister Jean Chrétien, who was so confident in a Clinton win, that he was bashing Trump in late October, mere days before the election.

"When Hillary had pneumonia, there are pills to help you against pneumonia, but apparently there is no pill against something like stupidity," he said. Chrétien called Trump "unbelievable," and said he was "taking away the dignity of public life."

When the new boss and the old boss of the Liberal Party feel comfortable disparaging the Republican candidate, it's no surprise that so many other Liberals joined the fray.

Roland Paris, a senior foreign policy advisor to Trudeau, called Trump "odious." Scott Brison, the president of the Treasury Board, mocked Trump's "toupee." Carolyn Bennett, Trudeau's Indian Affairs minister, tweeted that it was "concerning" that some Americans had voted in advance polls, before a decade-old audio tape of Trump's locker-room talk with a U.S. journalist was released. Bennett is a busy cabinet minister, in charge of the welfare of more than 600 Indian reserves. But she made time to become a self-styled U.S. political pundit, cheering along as late-night comedians mocked Trump, or as other Republicans criticized him, even claiming that Trump bragged about "sexually assaulting women."

That extreme allegation was picked up by Trudeau himself,

who did a press scrum where he used the phrases "sexual harassment" and "violence against women" when asked about "the issue of the American election."

With Trudeau practically accusing Trump of rape, other cabinet ministers' comments seem pale by comparison. John McCallum, the immigration minister, trumpeted support for Canada's open-door policy towards Syrian refugees, while bashing Trump's plans. Trudeau himself went on the CBS show *60 Minutes* to criticize Trump's immigration plans, which he described as "big walls and oppressive policies."

But even that sort of language wasn't critical enough for some. Journalist Rosemary Barton flew down to Washington, D.C., with Trudeau in 2016 as the campaign was heating up. Barton asked: "I'm wondering why you don't speak out more forcefully against some of the things [Trump] has said, which run counter to anything you believe. Anti-Muslim rhetoric, anti-woman rhetoric, building walls against people — why don't you say what you actually think about him?"

It's presumptuous for a reporter to claim to know the secret thoughts of a political leader, but in Barton's case, she probably did — Barton isn't an independent journalist, but rather an employee of the CBC, Canada's state broadcaster. She has a familiar way with Trudeau — the two of them famously posed for a fan/hero selfie shot before the interview was filmed.

Perhaps Barton was simply looking to make some news, like her private-sector competitors at Maclean's magazine did. When they asked him about Trump, Trudeau called it "the politics of division, the politics of fear, the politics of intolerance or hateful rhetoric. If we allow politicians to succeed by scaring people, we don't actually end up any safer. Fear doesn't make us safer. It makes us weaker."

That's not a politician going rogue, or forgetting his lines. That's what Trudeau really feels. Or as Trudeau's life-long friend, mentor and principal secretary, Gerald Butts, put it so subtlely on Twitter, "I wonder how many people are searching the world's databases for a picture of Trump and Duke right now."

That's a level of partisanship that is rare for politicians of one country to use to comment about politicians in another — let alone for senior Canadian officials to use to describe a major party's presidential candidate. It speaks of a deep personal and political connection between Canada's Liberal Party and the U.S. Democrats.

The Democrats have gone through their various stages of grief since November 8 — from staging street protests against the election result, to filing legal recounts in key states, to blaming everyone from the FBI to the KGB. Most Democrats have now made their peace with Donald Trump becoming president; but the Canadian wing of the Democrats — called the Liberal Party of Canada — hasn't got the memo. Like Japanese soldiers in the Philippine jungles still holding out hope for a victory years after Tokyo's surrender, there's something admirable about the undying loyalty Trudeau and company have for the Clintons. But if they don't keep that passion tamped down deep inside, it's going to hurt Canada.

Trouble is, the anti-Trump insults that Trudeau and his cronies said during the U.S. election campaign have turned into anti-Trump actions that Trudeau has ordered the Canadian government to do.

◆

In the weeks after Trump's win, Trudeau visited Cuba and posed for pictures with Raul Castro, and sent a Canadian navy ship on a friendship mission to the island nation for the first time in more than 50 years. He announced $25 million in foreign aid to Gaza, which is run by the terrorist group Hamas. And he praised China's Communist leaders, even as tawdry reports of unethical fundraising by Chinese billionaires dominated Canadian headlines.

Weeks after Trump's election, Trudeau's chief of staff, Katie Telford, flew to a conference in California, where she crowed about the Canadian election and told U.S. executives to move to Canada — with their jobs. It was a provocative statement to make, given Trump's focus on repatriating jobs to the U.S.

It's possible for this sort of sniping to be buried in the past. Trump surprised many pundits, who had called him thin-skinned, by reaching out to former Republican rivals like Mitt Romney and Nikki Haley in the weeks after the election, and even to partisan Democrats from Al Gore to Mexican billionaire Carlos Slim, the chief investor in the *New York Times*. Trump may be easily offended, but he appears to be able to quickly patch thing up, too. The real question is: do Trudeau and the Liberals actually want a working relationship with Trump — or do they prefer to use him as a punching bag for their own political purposes?

TWO

THE END OF THIRD WORLDISM

Donald Trump did not win the election on foreign policy — that's not what flipped rust-belt states like Pennsylvania and Wisconsin into the Republican column for the first time since 1984. Trump's promise of bringing back jobs to America is what did it, with the help of an unlikable Democrat, of course. But in the age of globalization, bringing jobs back from overseas is a foreign policy in itself — it's the traditional use of foreign affairs as a means of pursuing America's national interests, not just making virtue-signalling speeches about global warming to international talk-shops like the United Nations.

Trump's slogan, "Make America Great Again," doesn't just mean prosperity. It means nationalism, too — national pride, independence and a foreign policy driven by national interests. When Donald Trump talked about China — which he does so much that the Huffington Post put together a three-minute video compilation of him simply saying "Chigh-nuh" again and again —

it may have sounded like he was talking about a foreign country, but he was really talking about manufacturing jobs in the U.S.

That's the opposite of the foreign policy approach taken by Justin Trudeau, his senior aide Gerald Butts and Trudeau's brother and self-styled foreign policy deep thinker, Alexandre "Sacha" Trudeau. To them, foreign affairs is also about symbolism, but their philosophy isn't about making Canadian interests paramount, or even projecting Canadian values abroad. It's about Canada being a naive do-gooder, unrelated to Canadian trade, military or cultural interests. It's a combination of impotence and social preening, perfectly summed up in the final words of Trudeau's UN speech, where he condemned Trump: "Canada is a modest country. We know we can't solve these problems alone. We know we need to do this all together. We know it will be hard work. But we're Canadian. And we're here to help."

Here to help whom?

Help Canadians, or foreign countries? Which foreign countries, and on what basis? With what principles in mind?

"We're a modest country" is pretty much the opposite of "Make America great again." It's not true, actually — Canada is a G7 country with an economy as large as Russia's — larger than South Korea, Argentina, the Netherlands and 190 other countries. We're NATO allies; we're a moral force for democracy, going back to the First World War. In what way is that modest?

Perhaps Trudeau meant it as false modesty — fishing for compliments, as he campaigned alongside the dictatorships of the world to regain a seat for Canada on the UN Security Council. Who knows? It's never a good idea to put more thought into a Trudeau speech than he himself has put into it. Better to look at the advisors around him and the decisions he has made — and perhaps look at the foreign policy track record of his father, Pierre Trudeau.

That's a very small circle — two people, really: Trudeau's best friend since university, Gerald Butts, and Trudeau's younger brother, Alexandre. Both of them are globalists who see loyal citizenship to one country as being tantamount to racism — they're internationalists, but of the sort who would rather do deals with illiberal dictatorships than with true allies. To them, foreign policy is a chance to demonstrate how open-minded they are, to signal how virtuous they are. The idea of pursuing national interests is absurd to them — they don't believe in nation states to begin with.

Justin Trudeau himself once boasted that he had visited 90 countries before becoming an MP — a nearly impossible number to reach, except as a perpetually rootless travel bum. His brother Alexandre went a step further — actually working for the foreign dictatorships of Iran and China, as a reliable propagandist for each of them.

Butts has travelled widely, too, but his trips were more businesslike: as the former president of World Wildlife Fund-Canada, Butts connected with the global environmental movement and helped funnel millions of foreign lobbyist dollars into Canada for anti-oil sands and anti-pipeline campaigns.

These men are the opposite of Trump in every regard, but it's who they truly are — and that's going to be a problem.

CUBA

Donald Trump would have won the election even without Florida, but it would have been nail-bitingly close. Florida's 29 electoral college votes make it the most important state up for grabs — only California and Texas have more, and neither state is competitive. Trump won Florida — a feat that neither Mitt Romney nor John McCain did — in part because of the strong support of Cuban-Americans. Fifty-four per cent of Cuban-Americans in Florida voted for Trump, a higher proportion than white people.

Trump earned their vote by criticizing Obama's appeasement of Castro — one-sided concessions that were given without any movement on human rights. Trump went to Florida the day before the election, pledging to "stand with the people of Cuba and Venezuela in their fight against oppression." That's pretty tough talk: other than when referring to Iran and North Korea, Trump hasn't used such scorching language against another country.

That's Trump.

Canada's Trudeau family has a love affair with Cuba's Castro family that goes back a generation. In the 1970s, Pierre Trudeau made an international scene of being the only NATO leader to openly pal around with the Communist dictator at the height of the Cold War. No surprise — Pierre Trudeau also loved Communist China, and once laughably referred to Siberia, in the Soviet Union, as the land of the future.

But all that was before the Berlin Wall fell and Communism was utterly discredited for all to see, not only as an economic system, but as a moral system, as well.

One of the last hold-outs though is the anachronism of Cuba, a prison island in the Caribbean where the Castro brothers have built an incredibly cruel regime, killing a similar proportion of their own countrymen as Josef Stalin did in the U.S.S.R.

The Castros appreciated Pierre Trudeau's loyalty and the endless propaganda victories he gave them — not only internationally, where Trudeau's disunity with western democracies undermined NATO's solidarity and resolve, but more importantly, at home, as proof of legitimacy. Imagine how desperate and demoralizing it would have been to democracy activists in Cuba to see their national jailer in carefully posed photo-ops with the Prime Minister of a democratic country like Canada. It's one thing for leaders of liberal democracies to ignore Cuban dissidents; it's another thing for them to actually shore up Cuba's dictator.

When Pierre Trudeau died in 2000, it wasn't surprising that the only two world leaders who attended his funeral were Jimmy Carter and Fidel Castro.

Trudeau knew what he was doing: he had been a Marxist since his university days; he had always been anti-American; and he fancied himself as some sort of white saviour of the Third World, not quite a Manchurian Prime Minister, but one who could always be counted on to tweak the nose or kick the shins of the United States.

Like father, like sons.

Trudeau's boys, Alexandre and Justin, inherited their father's fawning admiration for dictators. In a famous newspaper article that was more suited to a satirical website like The Onion than the *Toronto Star*, Alexandre praised Fidel Castro as a child might describe a superhero. In fact, he actually compared him to Superman: "His intellect is one of the most broad and complete that can be found. He is an expert on genetics, on automobile combustion engines, on stock markets. On everything. Combined with a Herculean physique and extraordinary personal courage, this monumental intellect makes Fidel the giant that he is. He is something of a superman."

He actually wrote that. And the Star actually published it.

And judging by Justin Trudeau's tenure as Prime Minister, the Trudeau brothers actually meant it.

Funny enough, Justin Trudeau waited until after Donald Trump's election as president to make his first state visit to Cuba, posing with Raul Castro for iconic propaganda pictures, just like Pierre Trudeau before him had done.

But it wasn't just a personal visit: Trudeau sent the first Canadian navy vessel on a friendship visit to Havana in more than 60 years and the navy's official Twitter account called the dictatorship an "island paradise."

But that was nothing compared to Trudeau's official statement on the death of Fidel Castro, shortly after his visit. It reads as if Alexandre wrote it — and maybe he did:

"It is with deep sorrow that I learned today of the death of Cuba's longest serving President.

"Fidel Castro was a larger than life leader who served his people for almost half a century. A legendary revolutionary and orator, Mr. Castro made significant improvements to the education and healthcare of his island nation.

"While a controversial figure, both Mr. Castro's supporters and detractors recognized his tremendous dedication and love for the Cuban people who had a deep and lasting affection for 'el Comandante.'

"I know my father was very proud to call him a friend and I

had the opportunity to meet Fidel when my father passed away. It was also a real honour to meet his three sons and his brother President Raúl Castro during my recent visit to Cuba.

"On behalf of all Canadians, Sophie and I offer our deepest condolences to the family, friends and many, many supporters of Mr. Castro. We join the people of Cuba today in mourning the loss of this remarkable leader."

Deep sorrow? Legendary? Love for the Cuban people?

Castro was a tyrant; a dictator who ordered the mass imprisonment and murder of his opponents. He pilfered his country's wealth, becoming a billionaire himself while his country suffered. Perhaps the most appalling words in that disgraceful statement was Trudeau co-opting Castro's critics and declaring that even they recognized his dedication to the Cuban people. Tell that to the estimate 15,000 enemies of the revolution that Castro had murdered, and the many more imprisoned for political crimes.

Trudeau laughably called Castro Cuba's "longest-serving president," as if that were an achievement earned at the ballot box, rather than power guarded jealously through secret police and prisons.

Trudeau's eulogy was so over-the-top, it made international headlines, particularly in the U.S., and it was seized upon by Cuban-Americans like Florida Senator Marco Rubio — just two weeks after Trump's election victory, before Trump and Trudeau had a chance to have their first meeting.

It's one thing for Canada to have an independent policy towards Cuba — Canada never submitted to America's economic embargo against Cuba and thousands of Canadians who can morally justify vacationing in a dictatorship travel there for cheap winter getaways each year. It wasn't that Trudeau had a different policy than Trump. It was that Trudeau's expression of his affection was so extreme, so far beyond the norms of diplomatic niceties. It was so personal, it could only have been written by Trudeau or his brother — not by some professional civil servant or diplomat.

Trump called Cuba a land of oppression. Trudeau called it a land of love. They can't both be right.

For Trudeau, Cuba is just another faraway Third World country that lets him play the role of a jet-setting internationalist. For Trump, it's an enemy dictatorship just 90 miles off the coast of Florida, and it's a key issue in the third-largest state in the union.

How far can Trudeau push his family's Castro fetish before Trump pushes back?

MEXICO

Without a doubt, the number one applause line in Donald Trump's campaign speeches was when he said he'd "build a wall" along the Mexican border.

He would talk about his wall lovingly; he'd get excited about it. "I will build a great wall — and nobody builds walls better than me, believe me — and I'll build them very inexpensively. I will build a great, great wall on our southern border, and I will make Mexico pay for that wall. Mark my words," went one typical iteration of the speech. In other versions, he talked about gates in the wall and about how high the wall will be. At Trump's rallies, men would come in hardhats with placards saying they were ready to work on building the wall.

Trump's campaign and the wall are inseparable. It's not just a talking point; whether that wall gets built — and how fast — will be taken as tangible proof of whether or not Trump means, not just what he says about immigration and illegals, but whether he means anything at all.

That wall is going to be built.

The wall has become a symbol of Trump's boldness and his willingness to take on sacred cows that no other politician would. But it obviously has a real function, too: to stop illegal immigrants from crossing into America.

Well, that's where Justin Trudeau decided to step in.

America's northern border is twice as long as its southern one. And that's not even including the long Canadian border with Alaska — all told, more than 5,500 miles, compared to the 1,933 miles with Mexico. The Canada-U.S. border is the longest undefended border in the world, a symbol of peace and harmony. If an American presidential candidate is campaigning on a border wall with Mexico, that's a very good time for Canada to stay quiet as a mouse, rather than courting trouble.

But Trudeau just couldn't help it. Maybe it's his Third Worldism; his lenient approach to immigration; or, just as likely, a passive-aggressive attempt to embarrass Trump in the middle of the election campaign. So on June 28, 2016 — just three weeks before the Republican convention in Cleveland, where Trump would be officially chosen as the party's candidate — Trudeau made a noisy announcement that Canada was going to abolish the requirement for Mexicans to get a visa before coming to Canada. In an official Government of Canada press release, Trudeau boasted that Mexican migrants could now come to Canada after a quick application "that takes just minutes to complete online" and costs $7. Trudeau made a point of personally announcing this decision — not leaving it to the immigration minister. He was making a point: he was the anti-Trump.

The policy decision made no sense: non-partisan civil servants warned Trudeau in an internal memo that removing the visa requirement would cost Canada more than $400 million in increased law enforcement and other costs associated with a coming wave of bogus refugees.

The visa requirement had been put in place in 2009, precisely because of a wave of bogus asylum claims by illegal Mexican migrants. So what? It was a chance for Trudeau to show how out-of-fashion Trump was.

And, as with Canada's policy toward Cuba, even after Trump won the U.S. election, Trudeau wasn't about to stop triangulating against Trump. Right after the election, Trudeau reached out by phone to coordinate policy on the NAFTA free-trade agreement. But he didn't reach out to Trump; he reached out to the Mexican president, so the two of them could form a united front against Trump.

There's nothing wrong with consulting with another country, especially one with which Canada has a trade agreement. But how is it in Canada's interests to team up against the U.S.? It's in Mexico's interests, but why would Canada want to get involved in another country's fight? Mexico is an unimportant market for Canada — it buys just $6 billion/year in goods and services, compared to 50 times that for the U.S. market. Other than solidarity with the Third World, what possible reason would

Canada have for synching up with Mexico, instead of with the U.S. itself?

CHINA

Justin Trudeau loves China. Not just its people, or its history, or culture, or language, or food. Those are things anyone could admire.

But Trudeau specifically loves a different part of China. "You know, there's a level of admiration I actually have for China because of their basic dictatorship," he told a group of Liberal activists at a campaign "ladies night" in 2013.

Trudeau admires the worst thing about China, the part of China that abuses Chinese people: its Communist dictatorship, the part of China that massacred its own citizens at Tiananmen Square.

The rest of Trudeau's impromptu declaration of love that night was remarkable, too. He told the Liberal ladies that China's dictatorship was precisely what was "allowing them to actually turn their economy around on a dime and say, 'we need to go green fastest, we need to start, you know, investing in solar'."

But China is the most polluted country in the world, not the greenest. According to a 2016 report from the World Health Organization, more than a million people a year die from air pollution alone in China; pollution costs China 6.5% of its GDP. Trudeau may think China is, "you know, investing in solar," but it's investing far more in coal — with its latest five-year plan calling for increased production and consumption of it. According to the Institute for Energy Research, "from 2005 through 2011, China added about two 600-megawatt coal plants a week, for 7 straight years. And, China is expected to add the equivalent of a new 600-megawatt plant every 10 days for the next 10 years."

Trudeau's desire to be loved by China sometimes expresses itself in very needy ways. During his state visit there, Trudeau ordered the Canadian government to buy huge billboards welcoming him to China, with a picture of him hugging a panda. It's a cute photo, but paying to put up "welcome" signs for yourself is a bit like sending yourself roses on Valentine's Day.

After Trudeau's visit to the G20 summit in China, Canada's trade minister, Chrystia Freeland, was asked by CNBC to list any successes Trudeau had achieved. Her gushing answer was that the Chinese had given Trudeau the nickname "Little Potato" — because his name rhymed with the Chinese word for potato. That's Trudeau on China: obsequious, desperate, unprofessional.

Just like his brother, Alexandre Trudeau. In a stunning interview in late 2016, Alexandre said that the Chinese government itself had commissioned a book from him — called *Barbarian Lost: Travels in the New China*. When you write a book for a foreign government, it's not a work of non-fiction; it's a work of propaganda. And Alexandre was only too happy to go along. As he told Ottawa Magazine, "I'm still an outsider there — a Barbarian — but what China has given me is a perspective on the West. From China, it's much easier to understand the West. I now look at our own freedoms with a little more circumspection and consider some of the irresponsible nature of some of the freedoms we enjoy."

The brothers agree: the lack of freedom in China is one of the best things about it.

Being free — like being a multi-party liberal democracy — why, that's just being "irresponsible." The Chinese certainly got their money's worth: Alexandre confirmed that his brother, Justin, "read it a week before he left for China and he told me it helped him get up to speed in what to think and feel about China." Forget about professional diplomats, civil servants and China experts — Justin Trudeau's brother was paid to write a propaganda brochure, and that's what the Prime Minister read before his big trip.

But there are professional China hands in Trudeau's government — in fact, his government is stuffed with China-connected businessmen. Peter Harder, the head of the Canada-China Business Council, ran Trudeau's transition team, which is largely about choosing senior appointees. Harder himself was then appointed as the government's leader in the Senate by Justin Trudeau. Harder is deeply connected with China's crony capitalists and the Communist Party itself. Before joining the Senate, he was a senior policy advisor to the global law firm Denton's, which has thousands of deal-making lawyers in China. Jean Chrétien, the former Liberal Prime Minister who occasionally advises Trudeau, also works at Denton's. Chrétien's son-in-law's company, Power Corp., has major investments there. It even built the controversial Beijing-to-Tibet railway. Chrétien himself has been a lobbyist in China ever since he left office, and Harder was on the board of Power Corp., too. It's all in the family — these are people who specialize in downplaying human rights issues, ignoring Chinese espionage in Canada and who love greasing the wheels for friends and family, so they can get rich in China.

So Alexandre Trudeau can write the love-letters; Harder and Chrétien can write the deals.

That's about 180 degrees different from Trump's approach to China. Trump's trade policy during his campaign had seven points to it — three of them were about China, and none of them would earn him the nickname Little Potato.

They're very simple. "Instruct the Treasury Secretary to label China a currency manipulator." That's probably gobbledygook to Trudeau, a former substitute drama teacher and snowboarder. But Trump — and every laid off factory worker — knows what it means: China's government artificially manipulates its currency to undercut American factories. The U.S. bought US$367 billion more from China in 2015 than it sold to China — that's a billion dollars a day going to factory workers overseas. It's a big deal in Canada, too, as China sold $46 billion more in exports to Canada than it bought in return. Not only does Trudeau not mind, he positively takes steps to keep it that way: by ripping up the National Energy Board's approval of the $10 billion Northern Gateway pipeline project, not only did Trudeau destroy the biggest shovel-ready infrastructure project in Canada, he permanently blocked exports of 550,000 barrels a day of oil to China — worth $9 billion a year when oil is at its lows, around $50/barrel, and $18 billion a year if oil gets back up to $100/barrel.

That one political decision that could literally have reduced Canada's trade deficit by a third.

Trump's second campaign policy regarding China reads: "Instruct the U.S. Trade Representative to bring trade cases against China, both in this country and at the WTO. China's unfair subsidy behavior is prohibited by the terms of its entrance to the WTO." That's as close to a declaration of a trade war as is possible for a campaign platform. And just by writing it, Trump is sending a signal, not only to the Chinese government, but also to manufacturers in China, that they shouldn't expect the status quo to continue. Perhaps it's a coincidence, but just one week after Trump's election, Apple Inc. announced that it was looking at moving its iPhone production to the United States.

The third China policy was the toughest of them all — a threat to punish China for stealing U.S. industrial secrets: "Use every lawful presidential power to remedy trade disputes if China does not stop its illegal activities, including its theft of American trade secrets."

Trump has railed against Chinese commercial espionage before; in 2013, he tweeted, "As China is built on corporate espionage, currency manipulation & cheap labor, its economy is a ticking time bomb." That was a frustrated business leader musing out loud. His campaign platform — which went on to list U.S. trade laws he would rely on to punish China — is a lot more specific and a lot more serious.

Canada's spy agency, CSIS, has publicly estimated that there are 1,000 Chinese spies in Canada, mainly engaged in economic espionage. When the Conservatives dared to mention that, China reacted viciously. Trudeau learned his lesson. He won't do anything like Trump, and he won't even say anything like Stephen Harper. His strategy is: go along to get along. In August 2016, Trudeau tweeted: "A stable, constructive relationship with China is our priority." That suits Peter Harder, Jean Chrétien and the boys at Power Corp. — nobody wants to rock the boat when things are going great. But when 1,000 Chinese spies are stealing Canadian technology — including hacking that reportedly led to the collapse of the Canadian high tech company Nortel — a "stable" continuation of the status quo isn't acceptable.

Donald Trump has put China on notice that things are going to change. Trudeau has said he doesn't want things to change — not on trade deficits, and not on corporate spying.

Not on human rights, or democracy, either.

Trump outraged China — and the China lobby in North America — by taking a phone call from Taiwan's democratically elected president, Tsai Ing-wen, shortly after the U.S. election. Trump not only publicized the phone call on Twitter, he shot back at his critics: "Interesting how the U.S. sells Taiwan billions of dollars of military equipment but I should not accept a congratulatory call." By contrast, Justin Trudeau appointed Yuen Pau Woo, a Malaysian-born apologist for Communist China, to the Canadian Senate. In his maiden speech, Woo condemned a Senate motion that dared to criticize China for its territorial aggression in the South China Sea, which included building an artificial island that's loaded with military systems. The world has condemned that provocative move by China, including in a unanimous ruling by an international tribunal in The Hague. But to Trudeau's appointee, Senator Woo, the real threat to peace wasn't China's military build-up, but rather the Canadian Senate even mentioning it: "A dogmatic and trenchant insistence on international law could … be the very precipitant of conflict," he said.

If Donald Trump declares a trade war against China — and pushes back against Chinese expansionism in the region — which side will Justin Trudeau put Canada on?

Or will he have to ask Peter Harder first?

IRAN

If the sheer number of Twitter comments are anything to go by, Iran is the country that vexes Donald Trump more than any other, except China. And like China, Trump has been thinking about American policy towards Iran for a long time.

"Iran's nuclear program must be stopped – by any and all means necessary," he tweeted back in 2011. Not a lot of room for interpretation there. There are dozens of comments like that, such as this call for a military strike against Iran: "Why did Barack Obama liberate Libya and do nothing for the Iranian protestors? Iran is a threat to our national security." Or this one, hitting both China and Iran at the same time: "Our enemy China is illegally buying oil from our enemy Iran. China loves it!" Trump wants to negotiate with China. He's long past that with Iran: "While everyone is waiting and prepared for us to attack Syria, maybe we should knock the hell out of Iran and their nuclear capabilities?" Trump hasn't wavered after his election, either, calling Obama's nuclear deal with Iran "horrible," and telling Israel to hold on until he's inaugurated.

But while Trump openly muses about attacking Iran, Justin Trudeau and his Liberals are racing to normalize relations with the Islamic republic, even signing secret agreements with the country, despite Canada declaring it a state sponsor of terrorism and ending diplomatic relations in 2012.

In October 2016, Montreal Mayor Denis Coderre — a key Trudeau ally in Quebec — travelled to Iran to sign a secret agreement. No details about the agreement were released; in fact,

Coderre's trip to Iran was kept a close secret by the mayor and his office. News of it only seeped out when Iranian state media trumpeted Coderre for propaganda reasons.

The Liberal Party's love for Iran is being requited. In November 2016, Majid Jowhari, an Iranian-born Liberal MP from Richmond Hill, Ontario, hosted a delegation of Iranian MPs at his constituency office. The Iranian delegation also met with CAE Inc., a Montreal company that specializes in military aviation, including flight simulators. Like Coderre's secret trip to Iran, the Iranian delegation to Canada was kept secret by the Liberals, and only revealed by a Persian-language newspaper.

Jowhari isn't just hosting Iranian delegations. According to Iranian democracy activists, he's lobbying Canada on behalf of an Iranian airline called Mahan Air, which has been sanctioned by the U.S. for aiding terrorist groups. Jowhari wants Mahan Air to be able to fly to Canada, and has called for the lifting of all sanctions against Iran.

Trudeau himself hasn't publicly called for an end to the sanctions, but he's said he wants Canada to re-open its embassy in Tehran. And in an editorial board meeting with a pro-Iran newspaper in Toronto, Trudeau implied that the reason Stephen Harper's Conservatives had been so tough on Iran was simply to court the Jewish vote, saying that Harper's "positioning around Israel" was "very, very much focused on what is going to play well at the ballot box." Trudeau would probably say the same about Donald Trump, and called Barack Obama's nuclear deal with Iran an "excellent step."

It's one thing for Trudeau to pander to Iranian journalists, or to appease the Iranian-born MPs in his caucus. But Trudeau's most persuasive advisor — his brother, Alexandre — is a passionate Iran-booster who has worked for the dictatorship in a propaganda capacity.

Alexandre's specialty is making obscure, anti-western documentaries. None have done particularly well at the box office. But they're a useful guide for what the Trudeau family thinks about the world. He made an anti-American film called *Embedded in Baghdad* and an anti-Israeli film called *The Fence*. But his masterpiece on Iran, called *The New Great Game*, is particularly noteworthy. It's a fan's admiration for Iran and how it doesn't bow down to Israel or America. It sounds like a first year college student's regurgitation of a left-wing professor's talking points. But *The New Great Game* is different: it was made in cooperation with the Iranian government's official propaganda arm, Press TV (as well as other state broadcasters from the region, including Al Jazeera, which is controlled by the dictatorship of Qatar).

It's one thing for Canada and the U.S. to have a legitimate policy disagreement about foreign affairs. But Trudeau's affection for Iran is so personal, it's an emotional connection; one that's not driven by Canada's national interests. It's rooted in his brother's loving affection for Iran as the plucky Muslim country that has the courage to stand up to Israel and America. It's pushed by Trudeau's Muslim caucus, which is the largest in Canadian history. It's comprised of several Iranian-born MPs, including Maryam Monsef, the cabinet minister who claimed to have been an Afghan refugee, only to have it revealed that she was in fact born in Iran, and repeatedly travelled freely to that country — an unusual privilege that suggests friendly ties to Iran's government.

Donald Trump has repeatedly said he aims to crush the Islamic

State. But other than that rogue terrorist enclave, there is no other place on Earth with which Trump is more likely to go to war than Iran. Of all the foreign affairs differences with the U.S., this is the one most likely to come to a crisis the soonest.

ISRAEL

The Liberal Party has always had a split personality on Israel. On the one hand, for a generation, the party's centre of gravity was Montreal, a city with a large and active Jewish community that disproportionately donated to the Liberals. Trudeau kept that tradition alive by appointing Stephen Bronfman, an heir to the Bronfman liquor family, as his chief fundraiser.

On the other hand, the Liberals have always had a streak of anti-Semitism and anti-Zionism in their foreign policy. It was the Liberal government of William Lyon Mackenzie King that had an unofficial policy of "none is too many" when it came to Jewish immigrants to Canada, including turning away boatloads of refugees fleeing the Holocaust. And in more recent years, the Liberal Party's Third Worldism sided with Arab dictatorships over Israel, the lone democracy in the Middle East — or, at best, chose the position of "honest broker" between that democracy and the terrorist groups opposed to it. Under the Liberals, Canada become famous for abstaining at the United Nations — refusing to side with Israel in wave after wave of resolutions condemning the Jewish state.

There's a new factor at play now, too: while the Jewish

population of Canada remains static at around 350,000 people, the Muslim population has soared to over 1.3 million — more than doubling since 9/11. That demographic imbalance is showing up in the Liberal caucus, as well: in 2015, the Liberals elected ten Muslim MPs, including Omar Alghabra, the former president of the explicitly anti-Semitic Canadian Arab Federation. The Liberal Jewish caucus includes just six MPs. Those numbers will only become more lopsided over time.

Stephen Harper's pro-Israel credentials had earned him significant support among Canada's Jewish community, including from traditionally Liberal supporters. So Justin Trudeau made the conscious decision not to compete against Harper; but rather to concede the Israel vote to Harper and zero in on the anti-Israel vote.

In his campaign to become Liberal leader in 2013, Trudeau assiduously courted the Muslim vote, crisscrossing the country, going mosque to mosque, with Alghabra as his Muslim lieutenant. Trudeau would boast about all the mosques he had visited, rattling off their names with pride — including Montreal's controversial Assuna Wahhabi mosque, which is listed by the U.S. government as a place where Al Qaeda has recruited terrorists. Even after that mosque was revealed in a CBC investigation to be preaching extremist and violent messages, Trudeau stood by his decision to campaign there — and at other extremist locations. Trudeau wouldn't just attend mosques as a respectful outsider; he'd sometimes dress up in a full desert-style abaya, a flowing gown more suited to an Arabian desert than the Canadian tundra. And he'd actually join in Muslim prayers, including the Shehada — a prayer that, if Trudeau actually said it and meant it, would meet the sharia requirement for conversion to Islam.

Of course, Trudeau is not a Muslim — nor does he follow any faith, including the Catholicism into which he was born. But he knows the symbolism of Islam. For Mother's Day in 2013, Trudeau circulated a bizarre photo of his own mother and wife wearing hijab-style veils over their heads. Trudeau surely didn't mean it — it was just another costume party for him, just as he dresses up in pink for gay pride parades. But the message he was sending to Muslims was crystal clear: after ten years of a pro-Israel Prime Minister, they finally had their candidate. And in 2015's federal election, the math paid off. Stephen Bronfman's Jewish money plus all the Muslim votes helped put Justin Trudeau into office.

Trudeau didn't immediately bolt from Harper's pro-Israel record. He didn't want to spook the Jews, especially his Jewish donors. As a senior Liberal advisor told the *Globe and Mail* two months after Trudeau's 2015 win, "first we want to make sure we've got the Jewish vote back."

That caution didn't last long. Trudeau soon put the Canadian ambassador to Israel, Vivian Bercovici, under a gag order, and his office began a whisper campaign against her, before finally firing her. Choosing a hand-picked ambassador is the prerogative of any Prime Minister. In fact, it would have been inappropriate for Trudeau not to have done so, given the policy changes he was about to put in place. It wouldn't have made sense to have a pro-Israel ambassador doing anti-Israel things.

Like announcing a $25 million gift to the UN agency that runs schools in the Gaza Strip, called UNRWA. On the face of it, that sounds like a humanitarian exercise that any Canadian could support — though plenty of Canadian parents might ask why their schools can't get more funding. But the UN schools in Gaza are overseen by Hamas, the terrorist group that runs Gaza as a dictatorship. And the UN schools themselves are often run by Hamas terrorist agents, who allow Hamas to store weapons, including sophisticated rocket launchers, in the schools themselves — not only to hide them, but to ensure that Israel does not attack them, for fear of hitting the children and teachers. Hamas, in other words, uses UNRWA schools as human shields. That's on top of UNRWA's explicitly anti-Semitic curriculum, which teaches the destruction of the Jewish state as casually as it teaches math and spelling.

In 2009, Canada scaled back its financial support for these schools in response to Hamas's terrorism against Israel, and cut it off completely in 2010. Trudeau's decision to come roaring back with $25 million was big news. But even bigger — or at least stranger — was Trudeau's timing. He had been Prime Minister for a year, yet he chose the week after Donald Trump's election to make the announcement. It was part of Trudeau's anti-Trump whirlwind — visiting Cuba, funding Hamas schools, praising China. It was a busy week. Why would he do this, other than as a passive-aggressive reaction to the defeat of his U.S. mentor and ally, Hillary Clinton?

Trump has specifically condemned U.S. foreign aid to Gaza, calling it a "bad move" that will only wind up in the hands of Hamas terrorists. But then again, Trump doesn't have senior party members like Alghabra, or Borys Wrzesnewskyj, who, when visiting Lebanon, actually said he "was ashamed to be a Canadian," and claimed that Israel had committed "state terrorism." And then there's Denis Coderre, the Liberal mayor of

Montreal who proudly marched in an anti-Israel parade where
Hezbollah terrorist flags were flown. They're hard to miss — they
actually have a picture of a machine gun on them. But hey, a vote's
a vote.

The Liberal Party's historical position of ambivalence between
Israel the democracy on the one hand, and Muslim dictatorships
and terrorist groups on the other, worked well enough when the
rest of the west's leaders were morally ambivalent, too. During
Bill Clinton's presidency, no foreign leader visited the White
House more frequently than Yasir Arafat, the terrorist leader of
the Palestinian Liberation Organization. Had Hillary Clinton won,
Barack Obama's anti-Israel stance would have continued, and
Trudeau would be right in sync with "world opinion." But that
didn't happen.

There's a new era now. In the dying days of his lame-duck
term, Obama ended decades of precedent and refused to veto
an anti-Israel resolution at the United Nations Security Council.
It was one last shot at Obama's nemesis, Israeli Prime Minister
Benjamin Netanyahu, and it immediately earned a rebuke from
Trump, who condemned Obama and told Israel to "stay strong"
until his inauguration. Obama's secretary of state, John Kerry, kept
at it, giving an hour-long rambling speech condemning Israel as
intransigent and "right wing." It was the diplomatic equivalent
of a tantrum, but it had an unintended result: Theresa May, the
new U.K. Prime Minister, publicly condemned Kerry in rather
undiplomatic language: "we do not believe that it is appropriate to
attack the composition of the democratically elected government of
an ally."

Why did she do it? Why did she weigh in to a fight that wasn't about her or the U.K.? The consensus was that it was May's way of reaching out to the incoming U.S. administration, to ingratiate herself with Trump, who was clearly incensed with Kerry and Obama. In a way, it was much ado about nothing — one politician objecting to the choice of words used by another politician. None of it was binding in any way; none of it meant anything real. But it was the United Kingdom's way of signalling to the U.S. that it was interested in restoring the famous "special relationship" between the two countries that had been stressed under the Obama administration.

Just like the U.K., Canada has its own interest in Israel and the Middle East. But there are indirect interests at play, too. The U.K.'s Prime Minister thinks it's important to be in line with U.S. policy. So far, Canada's Prime Minister disagrees.

SAUDI ARABIA

Saudi Arabia isn't a particularly important country to Canada; it exports some oil to our East Coast refineries and will continue to do so as long as environmental extremists prefer tanker ships full of OPEC conflict oil to pipelines full of Canadian ethical oil. And Saudi Arabia buys military equipment from Canada, including a $15 billion armoured vehicle deal, negotiated under the Conservatives and continued by the Liberals.

America's relationship with Saudi Arabia is much deeper: the U.S. has imported trillions of dollars worth of Saudi oil over the years and, until recently, the U.S. military guaranteed the dictatorship's security with military bases on Saudi soil. American ships continue to patrol the dangerous waters of the Persian Gulf, acting as unpaid escorts for Saudi oil tankers.

American obsequiousness towards Saudi Arabia is bi-partisan. There is a Saudi tradition of giving enormous donations to U.S. presidents of both parties when they retire. These are styled as gifts to their presidential libraries, but they're really a delayed bribe. In the case of Hillary Clinton, the funds were paid in advance — the Kingdom of Saudi Arabia "donated" $25 million to her family's foundation in the run-up to her presidential campaign. No big deal — at $50/barrel, that's about 12 hours worth of Saudi oil sales to the U.S., a small price to pay to get in good with the next president.

That's certainly what the Saudis thought — and they must have been excited that Clinton's closest aide and advisor, Huma Abedin, grew up in Saudi Arabia, and even worked in the family business, editing their pro-Muslim Brotherhood journal.

Like everyone else, the Saudis thought Clinton and Abedin had the election in the bag; Donald Trump was so obviously going to lose. So it was safe for the Saudi royal family to join in the social media shaming of Trump — it was just so fun and tempting. It was the opposite of politically risky: it would cement the Saudis in Clinton's good books.

So no one less than Prince Al-Waleed bin Talal — a billionaire businessman, the grandson of the first king of Saudi Arabia and half-nephew to all the kings since — chose to make a smart investment: he was going to shame Donald Trump on Twitter, to please the Clintons.

"You are a disgrace not only to the GOP but to all America. Withdraw from the U.S. presidential race as you will never win," he wrote, apropos of nothing. Nearly 20,000 people retweeted that outburst. But he wasn't done yet. After Barack Obama made a pro-Muslim speech, Al-Waleed tweeted, "President Obama Your mosque speech shames Donald Trump comments against 1.4 billion Muslims. Thank You for Your wise leadership."

Back in the deserts of Saudi Arabia, when a billionaire prince insults you, you bow down and say "thank you," if you say anything at all. They don't have a lot of freedom of the press over there and they certainly don't talk back to their "royalty." It's a bit different being a brash billionaire in New York, where being mouthy is part of the civic identity and no one is above criticism. And Donald Trump — well, in a city of trolls, he's Yoda. "Dopey Prince Alwaleed Talal wants to control our U.S. politicians with daddy's money. Can't do it when I get elected," Trump tweeted back. And then he added a zinger: "Has your country, Saudi Arabia, taken ANY of the Syrian refugees? If not, why not?"

It's not just classic Trump — tit for tat, with massive retaliation. That's about self-respect, and the respect that Trump demands from others. That's a style — very different from Barack Obama's very famous deep bow to the King of Saudi Arabia when they first met. Donald Trump bows to no one, as no American has done since their Revolutionary War.

But it's also a sign that the status quo — the cozy U.S.-Saudi diplomatic relationship since the 1940s — is over. And as Trump fires the starter pistol for an American oil and gas renaissance, the economic relationship is about to change, too.

Whose side will Justin Trudeau be on?

CHRISTIANS

Donald Trump isn't a particularly devout Christian. During the campaign, he gave a speech at a Christian university and quoted a Bible chapter, pronouncing it "two Corinthians,"as it was written, not "second Corinthians," as it's commonly spoken. That would be like pronouncing the "j" in "hallelujah" — people might think you've never actually heard the word spoken before. It would have been fodder for more liberal late-night TV comedians, but of course they had never been to church to hear it pronounced properly, either.

Trump's approach to Christianity is probably the same as Winston Churchill's, who said he wasn't a pillar of the church, but a buttress — he supported it, but from the outside. For Trump, going back years, that has meant standing up for religious Christians who are being persecuted throughout the Muslim world. "Another radical Islamic attack, this time in Pakistan, targeting Christian women & children. At least 67 dead, 400 injured. I alone can solve," he tweeted in 2016, with characteristic showmanship. But the thing is, Christian victims of Islamic terrorism have had precious few public champions — even the Pope himself has been reluctant to publicly raise the subject.

Trump has made it a focus of his. When Saeed Abedini, a Christian pastor (who was a convert from Islam), was jailed by Iran for the crime of setting up churches, Trump made it his personal mission to have him released. For two years, Trump promoted his cause, meeting with the pastor's wife, giving her publicity, demanding that Barack Obama include Abedini's release in any negotiations with Iran. Trump's main PR weapon was his Twitter account, where he raised Abedini's issue no fewer than 14 times. It wasn't just a passing fancy.

Justin Trudeau takes the opposite approach. We are witnessing a genocide in the Middle East, committed by Muslim extremists and targeting not only Christians, but also other minorities, like the Yazidi people. Under Stephen Harper, and particularly Conservative immigration minister Jason Kenney, these persecuted minorities were given preferential immigration status. But Trudeau's campaign strategy was the opposite of Harper's. Harper already had a lock on the Christian vote — so Trudeau was going for the Muslims.

At a campaign stop in Toronto just ten days before the 2015 election, Trudeau was asked if he'd continue Harper's policy of favouring persecuted minorities. Trudeau's reply was blunt: "absolutely not," he said, calling Harper's approach "disgusting." He meant it.

Not only did Trudeau withdraw Canada's CF-18 military jets from the war against the Islamic State terrorists, he refused to even call the systematic murder of Christians by ISIS a genocide. Even John Kerry, the U.S. secretary of state, said that ISIS was committing genocide — against Yazidis, Christians and even against Shi'ite Muslims. Months later, Trudeau recanted and grudgingly agreed that the Islamic State was trying to wipe out Yazidis; but he specifically refused to acknowledge that Christians were being victimized — even though the Islamic State had released snuff movies of their terrorists slitting the throats of Christians in an elaborately staged ceremony, where the goal of ending Christianity was explicitly described.

There is no symbolic statement Trudeau won't read and no apology that he won't freely give — expressing emotions is his thing. But he becomes suddenly hard-hearted when it's Christians who need help. Denying that Christians are suffering from an Islamic genocide seems particularly stingy, but in the end, it's only symbolic. In a shocking announcement in December 2016, Trudeau restricted private sponsorship of Middle Eastern refugees to 1,000 people, even as he continued to flood Canada with government-chosen refugees. On the face of it, that surprise announcement makes no sense: if Trudeau wants to bring in tens of thousands more refugees from war-torn Syria, why wouldn't he allow private families and community groups to get involved — to raise money to cover the costs and, most importantly, to personally commit to helping to integrate those new arrivals once they land? If Trudeau wanted more Syrians, why wouldn't he let Canadians help?

The answer is shocking, but not surprising: it's because privately sponsored Middle Eastern refugees are disproportionately Christian Arabs. Christians are not only being attacked by the Islamic State in their villages. Even if they make it to a United Nations refugee camp, they're often attacked by other refugees who themselves are Islamic extremists, with the tacit approval of UN refugee camp staff who are overwhelmingly Muslim themselves.

It's those Christian refugees — refugees twice; once from the Islamic State and again from the UN system itself — that local community groups in Canada tend to support, especially churches. And it's those groups that Trudeau is limiting. There will be tens of thousands of Syrian refugees who pour into Canada in 2017. But Trudeau will ensure that as few as possible are Christian. It's almost like the old Liberal policy about Jewish refugees during the Second World War has been brought back, but this time it's about Christians. For Trudeau, "none is too many."

UNITED NATIONS

The opposite of "Make America great again" isn't usually phrased as "Make America weak," at least not in public. That sounds too disloyal for American politicians to say, and it sounds too hostile for foreigners to say.

No, the opposite of "Make America great again" is "Make the United Nations great." If you can do that, by necessity America is going to be made less great. It's a zero-sum game: militarily, diplomatically, financially — and most importantly, democratically. A powerful, globalist government, dominated by Third World dictatorships would by definition take decision-making away from sovereign countries, especially the world's sole hyperpower, the United States. More to the point, it would replace decisions made following the values of the U.S. Constitution, with decisions made in back rooms by rootless, unaccountable diplomats and lobbyists, most of whom come from less-free countries. The United Nations already ties the U.S. down with a hundred little treaties and resolutions, like Gulliver in Lilliput.

Donald Trump wants less of that. Justin Trudeau wants more of it.

Trudeau's maiden speech to the UN felt like a campaign appearance — he was trying to woo the ambassadors of the Third

World, or at least the scant few who sat through his speech. And it was a campaign appearance: Canada is not a permanent member of the UN Security Council, and so dozens of little countries have to be wooed one at a time for their votes, in order to get a seat on that panel. And being a good Liberal, Trudeau knows that the best way to campaign is to promise cash. In his first 100 days as Prime Minister, Trudeau gave away $4.3 billion in foreign aid: $13 million for Vietnamese farmers; $15 million for job training in Africa; $14 million for infrastructure in Indonesia; and a whopping $2.65 billion for global warming projects in the Third World. It just doesn't stop — while Alberta's oil industry wrestles with massive unemployment, Trudeau pledged $200 million in aid to the OPEC nation of Iraq.

It is sometimes in the legitimate national interest of a country to give foreign aid. But with Trudeau, it's the opposite — he first decides he's going to give the money away and the rationale follows later. Same thing with the deployment of Canadian military personnel. At their summer 2016 caucus retreat, the Liberals committed to spending $450 million for peacekeeping, and to sending 600 Canadian troops into harm's way. The particular country where the soldiers will be sent, or the particular mission? That hasn't been decided yet.

It's not about results; it's about optics. Foreign aid and even the deployment of soldiers is now about "Building on 'Brand Trudeau'." According to a document obtained by the Canadian Press through an access to information request: "There is significant enthusiasm at the global level for the messages conveyed by the Prime Minister. Canada could capitalize on this enthusiasm by investing in inclusivity, including through a robust

National Action Plan on Women, Peace and Security." So it's
not even about Canada; it's about other countries' enthusiasm.
It's not about making Canada richer or safer; it's about virtue-
signalling and buzzwords. To Trudeau and his inner circle, that's
what foreign affairs are — meetings with other elites from other
countries, in trendy places like Davos, Switzerland. It's endless
TED Talks about "inclusivity," followed by after-parties with
politically "woke" musicians and actors.

It's easy to see the appeal of that jet-set, especially to cosseted
trust-fund babies like Trudeau and his entourage. New York
or Switzerland are more glamorous than the rubber-chicken
circuit through Sudbury, Ontario, or Red Deer, Alberta. And all
that matters is political fashion — not results. It's the fun side of
politics, especially if you come with cash, as Trudeau always does.

It was the same way with Barack Obama, who was nominated
for a Nobel Peace Prize mere weeks after his election, but during
his term, the U.S. bombed seven countries and was never not at
war — a first for any U.S. president. Obama's two secretaries of
state set records for the number of miles flown around the world,
but few would say that the world is more peaceful now than when
he took office.

It's not just about the champagne and the hobnobbing, though.
There's an underlying ideology to it: the United Nations is anti-
nationalist and anti-western.

It's easy to see why. Born in the aftermath of the Second
World War, it's easy to understand why the UN was designed as
a counterweight to the excesses of nationalism. And when each
country in the world counts the same at the UN — at least in the
General Assembly, and in so many treaties and committees — it's

easy to see why the world's countless little tyrannies might try to coalesce against the mighty western democracies. Or at least try to extract the maximum amount of cash and other concessions from them.

That suited Barack Obama just fine. He inherited an anti-western bias from his father, Barack Obama Sr., the anti-colonialist exchange student from Kenya. Obama was explicitly against the idea of American exceptionalism — the idea that America is by nature first among nations. At a NATO conference in 2009, Obama was asked if he believed America was exceptional. He paused and said, "I believe in American exceptionalism, just as I suspect that the Brits believe in British exceptionalism and the Greeks believe in Greek exceptionalism." But life, and foreign policy, doesn't work that way; that's like giving everyone who runs a race a participation medal. Just because Obama wants a *Star Trek*-style future of total harmony and equality doesn't mean that China, Russia or Iran do, too.

Donald Trump hates the UN — or at least what it's become. "The United Nations has such great potential but right now it is just a club for people to get together, talk and have a good time. So sad!" reads one of his tweets on the subject since his election. Trump sees the UN as an obstacle to peace, not the path to it. After the UN voted to condemn Israel in December 2016, Trump wrote, "The big loss yesterday for Israel in the United Nations will make it much harder to negotiate peace. Too bad, but we will get it done anyway!" signalling that he will go around the UN, rather than work through it. Trump knows that only global jet-setters, or those elites who aspire to be a part of that club, value the UN these days — to most Americans, it's an expensive talk shop. "If the UN unilaterally grants the Palestinians statehood, then the US should cut off all its funding. Actions have consequences," he wrote back in 2011. He mocked the UN's obsession with nit-picking the west, instead of dealing with crises in the Third World: "Now the UN is attacking Redskins franchise. With all the world's problems, is this really a top priority?" he tweeted after the UN Human Rights Council put aside less pressing matters, like Syria and China, to focus on a football team's name.

If you're a modern progressive feminist multiculturalist — and Trudeau would certainly agree to each of those adjectives — the UN is morally superior than any individual country. To such a man, any national cultural identity would be recast as racist. Putting the national interest first would be unnecessarily competitive, even hostile. Standing up for one's own country, instead of joining in a globalist mesh, would come across as heretical. But Trudeau is in fact the Prime Minister of a country; how does he square it?

According to a gushing interview he did with the *New York Times* just days after the 2015 election, Trudeau has decided that Canada doesn't in fact have a core identity. Canada's history, language, values — all of that is part of some old-fashioned past. Now we're the perfect modern post-national state, like something out of the movie *Metropolis*.

"There is no core identity, no mainstream in Canada. There are shared values — openness, respect, compassion, willingness to work hard, to be there for each other, to search for equality and justice. Those qualities are what make us the first postnational state," Trudeau told the *Times*.

But those are emotional states — what kind of people wouldn't claim to seek justice or "be there for each other"? That's a Hallmark card cliche, or a friend's inscription in a high school yearbook. It doesn't describe a nation's characteristics. Canada has a 400-year history and many deeply held values — some of them enshrined by Trudeau's own father in the Charter of Rights and Freedoms. That document outlines Canada's dedication to fundamental freedoms, like freedom of speech and of the press. These are not universal ideas; they're actually part of a rare and valuable identity that took centuries to achieve. Freedom and democracy are not what you would get if you poured the essence of 200 UN member states into a big blender. Trudeau's harsh reaction to Conservative leadership candidate Kellie Leitch's insistence on screening would-be immigrants for essential Canadian values is part of this same moral relativism. But even that isn't completely coherent — aren't Trudeau's vague allusions to "equality" a sort of value?

Oh well — it's all just for show, it's all just for good PR, for glowing headlines in vanity newspapers around the world and hopefully some votes at the popularity contest for a UN Security Council seat. Nothing means anything anymore in a post-national, post-modern world.

That's one way of looking at the world. The other is that countries are different and some are better than others, and that a core duty of a country's leader is to promote its own interests. That's Trump, that's what "Make America great again" means and that's what Trump is going to do, with or without the UN.

THREE

CARBON IS COOL AGAIN

Donald Trump is a builder, which is psychologically closer
to the energy industry than the background of most politicians.
You can't build a skyscraper without plenty of steel and concrete,
which are brought in by truck, and originally were minerals mined
out of the Earth. Building is energy intensive. It's real life, done
by guys in hard hats. Pretty opposite from the world of Justin
Trudeau, the former drama teacher, and his professor friends.

Trudeau appointed as his natural resources minister Jim Carr,
a Member of Parliament from Winnipeg — not exactly an energy
town. Carr's a career politician, who before entering politics was a
musician who played an oboe, an instrument similar to a clarinet.

That's his background for handling one of the most
complicated, economically strategic departments in Canada. What
could go wrong?

Energy is one of Canada's most controversial issues right
now, with the oilsands in economic duress — partly from low

world prices, but mainly from anti-oil policies promoted by environmental lobbyists and enforced by anti-oil politicians. Trudeau himself is in that category — he campaigned against approving the Northern Gateway pipeline, a $10 billion, shovel-ready construction project that would have shipped 550,000 barrels a day of oil to the West Coast. It would have immediately become Canada's largest infrastructure project; and when complete, it would have cut Canada's trade deficit with China almost in half. That pipeline was approved by the National Energy Board after the most exhaustive review in Canadian history — and the approval came with 209 extra conditions. Despite that, Trudeau campaigned against it, saying not only would he rip up the contract's permit, but he'd also ban oil tanker traffic off the north coast of British Columbia.

Strangely enough, Trudeau continues to allow OPEC oil tankers to ship conflict oil to Atlantic Canada and Quebec. Only tankers carrying ethical oil exports to Asia are banned.

Carr is the natural resources minister in name. But in reality, all the key decisions on that file are made by Catherine McKenna, the social justice lawyer appointed as Trudeau's minister for "environment and climate change" — the title itself shows how the portfolio has been weaponized against the oil industry. This isn't about keeping lakes and rivers clean, or getting rid of the smog in big cities. It's about taking on the oilsands. It's unlikely Carr would ever have been an influential minister to begin with, but he was marginalized by Trudeau from the very beginning. Canada is by far the largest source of U.S. oil imports; yet when Trudeau flew with his enormous entourage to a gala dinner at the White House, Carr wasn't invited along. Nine other ministers were there.

Trudeau's mother and his in-laws were there. Gerald Butts was there. The Liberal Party's chief fundraiser was there. But not Carr. Somebody had to stay home, to make room for Hollywood stars Mike Myers and Sandra Oh.

And of course, the greatest environmental activist in the Canadian government is Trudeau's own principal secretary, his best friend since university, Gerald Butts.

Butts is the radical environmentalist who was the driving force behind Ontario's Green Energy Act, when he was a senior advisor to that province's premier, Dalton McGuinty. That law saw massive subsidies for experimental wind and solar power, in a province that had some of the cheapest electricity in the world — coming from the century-old hydroelectric dams at Niagara Falls and the largest clean coal-fired power plant in North America. Butts has moved on to bigger things, but according to Ontario's auditor general, the extra cost of shutting down economical fossil fuel-based energy and subsidizing eco-schemes was $37 billion by 2014, with another $133 billion to come over the next 15 years. That's $170 billion — or more than $30,000 for every household in Ontario. It's like another mortgage payment for families and it's forced many Ontarians into energy poverty.

Butts left Ontario politics to lead the extremist World Wildlife Fund-Canada, a foreign funded, anti-oil lobby group. While there, Butts popularized "Earth Hour," where people were literally encouraged to turn off all electricity for an hour — to sit in the dark, in the cold — as some sort of renunciation of industrial society. It never caught on; Canada is just too cold and too large a place to live without energy. But that wasn't ever really the goal: the goal was the demonization of energy, to redefine the use of electricity as some sort of sin, to condition people to think of it as an indulgence and prepare them for using less of it.

While at the WWF, Butts developed an international network of fellow travellers. He cultivated billionaire donors from around the world, including the radical, San Francisco-based Tides Foundation, New York's Rockefeller Brothers Fund and others. Butts was a charter member of the Rockefellers' "Tarsands Campaign," a multi-million dollar anti-oilsands pressure campaign that used propaganda and litigation to oppose Canadian oilsands production, pipelines and refineries.

It was while Butts was at the WWF that he issued his famous statement that the problem with pipelines like Northern Gateway wasn't any specific objection, such as the route of the pipeline, or any hypothetical risk of an oil spill. It was the fact that the pipeline had anything to do with oil at all: "the real alternative is not an alternative route. It's an alternative economy," he said.

Just that? Just the total overhaul of the entire economy — from cars and trucks, to airplanes and ships, to agriculture and industry, to home furnaces and factories? Butts' messianic zeal for destroying fossil fuels is one part centrally planned economics, one part alchemy-style fantasy science and one part lucrative lobbying. But it's been a disaster for Ontario homeowners and businesses, which have been saddled with the equivalent of a second national debt because of it. And now Butts and Trudeau have the whole country in their gun-sights.

Canada is blessed with the third-largest oil reserves in the world — 172 billion barrels, according to the U.S. Department of Energy's information agency. Only Venezuela and Saudi Arabia have more. By comparison, the United States is ranked tenth, with just 40 billion barrels of proven reserves. And no other country in the top ten is a liberal democracy. When it comes to ethical oil — oil that isn't controlled by OPEC dictatorships — Canada has half of the world's reserves. And Gerald Butts, Justin Trudeau and Catherine McKenna want to keep it in the ground.

That's Trudeau's approach to energy: he's stacked his government with environmental extremists, and he's made carbon taxes and global warming his signature issues.

Donald Trump? Put it this way: he nominated Rex Tillerson, the CEO of ExxonMobil, to be his secretary of state. Trump says he chose Tillerson for his experience and his leadership qualities — his oil background will likely be useful mainly in that Exxon took Tillerson to countless countries around the world, where he made real political and business connections. But appointing Tillerson shows Trump's complete disregard for the whims of political correctness. For Trudeau, it would be unthinkable to appoint an unabashed fossil fuels man as the country's chief diplomat — it would be like hiring a tobacco executive.

But Tillerson is just the beginning. Trump nominated former Texas governor Rick Perry as his energy secretary. Texas is well-known as an oil-producing state, but when Perry was elected governor in 2000, oil production had been on a long, steady decline, producing just over a million barrels per day. By the time Perry left office in 2015, that number had tripled. Texas now produces more oil each day than most OPEC countries. That's the result of a free enterprise spirit and the proliferation of fracking technology. But it was Perry who kept the environmentalists and regulators at bay, unlike U.S. states such as New York, where fracking has been banned.

Like Tillerson, Perry is comfortable with oil and gas; he knows more about it than the junk science hucksters in the media and he's not likely to be wooed by noisy anti-oil lobbyists. But perhaps most obviously, Perry and Tillerson show Trump's executive style: hiring proven leaders in their field. He's not appointing oboe players or social justice lawyers to manage oil and gas policy.

Trump nominated lawyer Scott Pruitt to lead the Environmental Protection Agency. Pruitt is the attorney general of Oklahoma who just happens to be suing the EPA in court. Pruitt's lawsuit is technical: it alleges that the EPA's anti-energy regulations violate the jurisdiction of states like Oklahoma. They're a one-size-fits-all policy designed to attack the energy industry, particularly coal. Pruitt once compared the EPA's approach to a "gun to the head." The man who is suing the EPA will soon be running the EPA.

It's no small thing — the department employs 15,000 bureaucrats and has an $8 billion annual budget. It'll still exist, and it'll still be the world's largest, best-funded and most aggressive environmental enforcement agency. It'll just be focused on real pollution, not the fake, politicized pollution of carbon dioxide.

Any one of those three key appointments would be a strong statement of Trump's support for fossil fuels. But taken together, it's unmistakable: America is going to mine coal, frack oil and gas, and build as many pipelines as investors want to. The economic miracle of America's recent fossil fuel revolution — including in unexpected places like Pennsylvania's Marcellus gas fields — is going to continue, and with it will come cheap, plentiful energy.

That Pennsylvania energy boom is a major reason why Trump won the presidential election there, the first time a Republican has done so since 1988, and it's a perfect example of the difference between Trump and Trudeau when it comes to energy.

Pennsylvania has been part of the rust belt for a generation, as the state's old industries — coal and steel — were squeezed between cheap foreign competitors and environmental regulators set on demonizing heavy industry.

When Barack Obama was running for president in 2008, he told a liberal San Francisco newspaper about his hatred for fossil fuels: "If somebody wants to build a coal-fired power plant, they can. It's just that it will bankrupt them." And Obama wasn't just targeting the coal miners and coal-fired power plants — he had it in for energy users, too. "Under my plan ... electricity rates would necessarily skyrocket," he said. In 2016, Hillary Clinton doubled down in a televised debate, saying, "We're going to put a lot of coal miners and coal companies out of business."

Obama and Clinton were using the same kind of language used by Gerald Butts and Catherine McKenna — the language of United Nations bureaucrats and environmental activists that gets knowing nods in university faculty lounges, where the phrases "coal miners" and "steel workers" are an insult, political shorthand for Archie Bunkers that any self-respecting metrosexual politician would demonize.

Pennsylvania, with a football franchise called the Steelers, still voted for Obama — twice. But counties in the western part of the state, where fracking for natural gas started to sprout up, began trending Republican. Take Washington County, Pennsylvania. In the 2008 presidential election, the county split pretty much 50-50 between Republicans and Democrats. In 2012, as the fracking boom really took off, the county went Republican by a 13% margin.

By 2016, Trump won by a whopping 25% margin, or 24,000 votes. Pennsylvania tipped into being a red state by just 65,000 votes, so between Washington Country and other nearby fracking regions, it was the energy industry that did it. Pennsylvanians took Obama and Clinton at their word when they threatened oil, gas, coal and steel — and they saw how the Democrats have been the party that wants to ban fracking, too. Like Texas, Pennsylvania has had an economic renaissance, with 200,000 jobs created in the industry, and the abundance of cheap, clean natural gas has reduced energy prices for the average Pennsylvania family by $1,000/year. That's what won the state for Trump: whatever skepticism the people of the Midwest might have had for the brash Manhattan billionaire and reality TV star, they knew he wasn't going to shut down any factories or mines.

Fracking is one of those subjects that divides people socially — like pick-up trucks, hunting or Walmart. Blue collar people — people who work in the outdoors, people who wear hard-hats — know fracking is just the name of a drilling process, no scarier than anything you'd find in an industrial factory. But even a car can be made to sound scary to someone who has never opened up their hood to see the mysterious internal combustion engine inside. Combustion — does that mean it might catch fire?

But fracking was invented in the 1940s and has been done millions of times. Most natural gas in Canada is fracked. But the word itself sounds dangerous, even vulgar. An emotionally driven, low-information politician like Trudeau would obviously find that troubling.

Natural resources are mainly a provincial matter in Canada, but Trudeau has made his position clear: he supports a ban on the industry. In 2014, he told reporters that, "in terms of fracking and shale gas, we need to make sure that we have all the information, that there is proper science done." But "we" do have all the information — it's the 70th anniversary of fracking. It's far safer, for example, than coal mining, a hazardous occupation that continues to claim lives every year. It's easy to believe that Trudeau doesn't know anything about it, but do unemployed workers really need to wait until their Prime Minister does a Google search?

Trudeau is never short of excuses for why energy projects can't proceed. With fracking, he says it needs more studying. But even after an energy project goes through a staggeringly long, independent review by experts, Trudeau can find a new excuse. The Northern Gateway pipeline proposal was first submitted to the National Energy Board in 2009 and it was painstakingly reviewed for five full years, with tens of thousands of pages of technical documents and countless witnesses appearing before an independent panel. There was an entire parallel process reviewing the pipeline through the lens of Aboriginal issues. Thousands of Canadians (and even foreigners) submitted testimony. The experts agreed: it was an environmentally safe, economically necessary project. And still Trudeau vetoed it.

So much for "the proper science." What business would spend five years applying to build a project in Canada, jump through every regulatory hoop at great cost and meet all the legal, scientific and environmental demands made of it, if it knew that at the end of the process, a whimsical Prime Minister might wave his hand, like some unimpressed Roman emperor at the Colosseum, and simply kill the project dead?

Trudeau doesn't really want to study fracking. He wants to

stop it — "studying" it is just an easier way to say so. Sometimes he doesn't even pretend to study something. After Trump's election, while Barack Obama was waiting for the moving vans to take his stuff out of the White House, Obama started going through his bucket list — things he couldn't do as president, that he might as well try to do, even in some symbolic way, in his last few days in office. So Obama, alongside Trudeau, issued an order banning any future drilling for oil and gas in the Arctic. It was just another of the hundreds of unilateral executive orders made by Obama, a controversial approach to governing increasingly used by him over the years, as he lost control over Congress. Whether or not Obama in fact had the legal authority to suddenly kill all drilling in Arctic will become a moot point the moment Trump becomes president. What was done by a presidential order can probably be undone by a presidential order. It wasn't true law-making by Obama; that takes time and effort, compromise and consultation. It was a pitiful act of showboating — one last attempt to get attention by a vain president concerned about his legacy.

But what's Trudeau's excuse? Why did Trudeau rent out Canada's oil and gas policy just to help his friend Obama with a PR stunt? How is that consistent with Trudeau's claims that he wants science-based policy?

Trudeau didn't even consult with the local communities, which were completely ambushed by the stunt. Obama was aiming one last rocket at Big Oil, but Trudeau hit northern Aboriginal communities, which rely on natural resource extraction for jobs. Canada's three northern premiers were only told about the announcement hours before it was made. Even the Liberal premier of the Yukon couldn't hold his tongue, denouncing not only the substance of the ban, but the way it was imposed on the north, as well.

Merven Gruben, the former mayor of Tuktoyaktuk, Northwest Territories, explained the price that would be paid for Trudeau's PR gift to Obama: "We're trying to be self-reliant and get off social assistance. You get all these environmentalists, and Greenpeace, World Wildlife Fund are doing all this stuff and shutting this down, and then they take off. They're not going to feed us." Gruben knows that the world's environmentalists simply use Aboriginals as cannon fodder — they don't really care about their welfare. What Gruben may not have known is that the former president of World Wildlife Fund-Canada, Gerald Butts, is Trudeau's best friend and principal advisor. That's all the consulting Trudeau needed to do.

Trump will repeal Obama's stunt ban. Trudeau probably won't. And that's the thing: it's almost a certainty that America is about to enter a golden era of energy production, whether it's coal, conventional oil and gas, or fracked oil and gas. Trump's energy policy platform from the election is strikingly simple: "Unleash America's $50 trillion in untapped shale, oil, and natural gas reserves, plus hundreds of years in clean coal reserves." And Trump takes dead aim at oil imports, too: "Become, and stay, totally independent of any need to import energy from the OPEC cartel or any nations hostile to our interests." And you can add to that Trump's promise of a major corporate tax cut and his stated support for pipelines like Keystone XL.

Trump's energy policy is explicitly hostile to conflict oil from OPEC countries. But unless Canada harmonizes its energy approach to America's, it's a sure thing that we'll get blindsided

◆

by Trump's energy nationalism, too. Ten years ago, before American fracking cut the price of natural gas by two thirds, a series of specialized ports were built along the Atlantic coast, for receiving massive tankers of liquefied natural gas (LNG) from OPEC countries like Qatar. After the ports were built, the increased production from Pennsylvania and other fracking states cut the price so low that imported gas couldn't compete. But those ports can be retooled to export natural gas and oil. And U.S. oil is already exported to Canada by rail — including oil fracked in North Dakota's Bakken Formation.

Right now, the United States is still the world's largest consumer of oil, and even with the fracking boom, it still imports millions of barrels each day. But every year that Canada's own oil industry is hobbled — whether it's environmentalists like Butts blocking pipelines, or oil investments being scared off by carbon taxes — is another year that the U.S. industry can catch up and meet that demand on its own. One day Canada's largest oil and gas customer will also become Canada's largest oil and gas competitor, as American tankers start to ship oil and gas overseas, going to the markets that just won't wait ten or twenty years for Canadian pipelines to be built.

But it's not just the oil and gas production itself that will move from Canada to the U.S. So will the jobs and the investments. It's happening already. Calgary, Canada's energy capital, has an unemployment rate of over 10%. In North Dakota, it's 3%, and it's not much higher in Texas. The world price for oil is the same; the difference is that companies in Alberta are scaling back their investment plans, or cancelling projects altogether, in response to anti-oil taxes and regulations that have been enacted already, and fears over what's still to come.

In December 2016, Norway's mighty Statoil company left Alberta. But at the same time, Statoil is investing in oil projects in Iraq — a country that announced seven new major oil and gas investments that month alone. It's incredible, but true: seven companies in one month decided that Iraq — home of the Islamic State terrorist group; a place where suicide bombers attack almost daily; neighbour of Iran, with its nuclear ambitions — is a less risky place to invest than Canada.

It's been months since Trump's win, but Trudeau and Butts are determined to keep pressing ahead with their carbon taxes and their enthusiastic adherence to global warming treaties that now seem about as meaningful as a high school Model UN club. Just days after Trump's election, Trudeau told reporters that, "one of the things people in Canada and indeed around the world understand is that there is tremendous economic disadvantage from not acting in the fight against climate change."

"Acting in the fight" is apparently a euphemism for Trudeau's carbon tax. But no one — not even Trudeau — seriously suggests that Canada's carbon tax on its own will make any difference at all to the world's climate. Trudeau's arguments are typically about showing goodwill and leading by example. But no other country in the world seems to be going along with Trudeau's economic self-sabotage. No other country has a carbon tax. Australia briefly implemented one, and repealed it just as quickly. Even Barack Obama didn't dare impose a carbon tax on the U.S., and Trump surely won't. What is the point of Canada doing so now, given Trump's clear plans to go in the opposite direction?

Trudeau's explanation got even stranger as it went on: "We

know that putting a price on carbon pollution is a way to improve our response to economic challenges, to create good jobs going forward and to show leadership that quite frankly the entire world is looking for, along with the solutions that go with it."

But that just doesn't make any sense: how does putting a tax on energy "improve our response" to anything, let alone "create good jobs"? Who told him that — his oboe-playing energy minister, or his social justice activist environment minister?

A few weeks later, Saskatchewan Premier Brad Wall had the temerity to point out the insanity of proceeding with a war on Canadian energy at the same time the U.S. unleashes its own industry. "Let's not be naive as Canadians. We need to be competitive with them," he said.

Trudeau didn't seem to have a reply rooted in economics or business, saying, "I think all Canadians know Canadian climate policy will be set by Canadians not by whoever happens to be president of the United States." That's obviously true; but it doesn't answer Wall's point about keeping up with our largest customer and competitor. And hadn't Trudeau just said that the real reason to have high carbon taxes was to somehow inspire other countries with our self-sacrifice? Wasn't the whole global warming scheme an international UN treaty, just Trudeau's favourite sort of thing anyways?

But that's what happens when the Prime Minister isn't a builder, has never signed the front of a paycheque and has never balanced a budget — either his own, or anyone else's. The United States is gearing up for the biggest energy boom since the time of John D. Rockefeller, and Canada wants to sit this one out. That's quite a decision for an energy-exporting country. For close to fifteen years, the oilsands and its exports is what kept the Canadian economy going — it was a source of high-paying jobs and countless contracts to firms across the country, ranging from engineers, to lawyers, to airlines. And of course there were the taxes and equalization payments that made sure Canada was the last G7 country to be hit by the Great Recession, and the first one to get out of it.

Letting all that idle in the name of a defunct UN treaty doesn't seem to be in Canada's national interest. The next election is less than three years away; it's possible Trudeau can finesse things by borrowing enough money to keep appearances up. But that can only last so long.

Gerald Butts's green schemes managed the impossible: to turn Ontario, once the economic engine of Canada, into a have-not province, our very own rust belt. Turning Alberta into the same thing might feel good to anti-oil extremists. But who does everyone think is going to pay the bills? If only Trudeau had a businessman in cabinet to ask for advice.

FOUR

CABINET MINISTER'S APPRENTICE

Two weeks before Donald Trump's inauguration, Justin Trudeau shuffled his cabinet. It was due for an overhaul anyways, but the prospect of sending as foreign minister the annoying professor, Stephane Dion — holder of a second French passport, coiner of the unforgettable whinge, "do you think it's easy to make priorities?" and creator of the appalling Green Shift carbon tax — to go head-to-head with Trump's secretary of state, Rex Tillerson — CEO of ExxonMobil; nickname: T-Rex — was just too painful for anyone to contemplate. Dion was relieved of the position, but has not yet taken his patronage consolation prize. He's probably still breathing into a paper bag, to stop from hyperventilating.

In his place, Trudeau has chosen Chrystia Freeland, the celebrity journalist. She's mastered the genre of the TED Talk — a short, prepared speech, heavy on futurism, packed with buzzwords, a dose of gossip and liberal smugness. Her most prominent book, *Plutocrats*, presents itself as a serious study of the world's richest people, but it reads like a college student trying to make a thesis out of Robin Leach's old TV show, *Lifestyles of the Rich and Famous*. She runs in celebrity circles herself, but more as a hanger-on. Even after she became a cabinet minster, she flew to Los Angeles to appear on Bill Maher's late-night talk show, directing her staff to find other government business to justify the taxpayer expense. Her one foray into business was a disaster; tapped by media giant Reuters to build an edgy website called Reuters Next, Freeland burned through more than $10 million, giving huge contracts to her friends, including one crafty consultant billing $300,000/month. It was a catastrophe, and when she suddenly quit to run for the Liberals, Reuters shuttered the whole project. Apparently it's easier to write gossip columns about successful businessmen, than to be one.

But to Trudeau, Freeland's shallowness and lack of business savvy were irrelevant; she was a high-energy woman who knew the "cool kids," whether in L.A., or Davos. And given that he needed to fill his quota of 50% female cabinet ministers, Freeland was a shoo-in; she was appointed minister of international trade. Her big foreign debut was accompanying Trudeau to the G20 summit in China. Canada left that meeting empty-handed, but Freeland gave a gushing interview to CNBC, where she boasted that the Chinese had given Trudeau a nickname: Little Potato. "We're quite proud," she told the stunned reporter.

The next month, Freeland followed up on this tour de force with a trip to Belgium for European free trade negotiations. Those can be difficult — they need a longer attention span than a

22-minute L.A. TV show, or a 20-minute TED Talk. At one impasse, Freeland stomped out of the meeting and held a press scrum where she was on the verge of tears, telling reporters through her sniffles that the European Union was being mean, especially "with a country as nice and as patient as Canada," and it wasn't fair, because she had worked "very, very hard" and hadn't seen her kids in days.

That's probably not a negotiating style Rex Tillerson has encountered as CEO of ExxonMobil, which has its own trade deals in more than fifty countries. Whether it was a sign of Freeland's deep insecurity and panic, or a deliberate negotiating strategy, is unclear.

But that's a problem with Trudeau's approach to cabinet-making: his appointments are based on appearances, not substance. And he's choosing from a caucus that itself was often chosen for reasons of racial or gender quotas.

That was a great fit with the race- and gender-obsessed Obama administration. When Barack Obama welcomed Justin Trudeau to the White House with a gala dinner, Trudeau brought his shiniest cabinet appointees, including Hunter Tootoo, the Inuit fisheries minister. When Obama visited Canada's Parliament, he gave a particular shout-out to Maryam Monsef, then the democratic reform minister, calling her "the girl who fled Afghanistan by donkey and camel and jet." That's what was important to Trudeau and to Obama — the back story, the romance, ticking the right politically correct boxes. Alas, Tootoo was sacked from cabinet for an ethics scandal and Monsef's entire biography has been proven a lie.

Left-leaning pundits — including quite a few in Canada —

have raged that Donald Trump's senior appointees are "old white men." That ignores leaders like Dr. Ben Carson, Betsy DeVos and Nikki Haley. But to the extent the criticism is true, it's not an accident. Trump is simply choosing his cabinet using different criteria: proven success in their field and experience in leadership positions.

Trudeau has boasted about the youth of some of his appointees — Karina Gould, who took over the democratic reform file from Maryam Monsef, is just 29; Bardish Chagger, the house leader, is a three-fer — she's a woman, she's Sikh and she's just 36. But once that box is checked and the celebratory press release is issued, then what? Gould's biography is paper-thin; she volunteered in a Mexican orphanage, worked as a low-level aide for a Washington, D.C., lobby group and volunteered a lot with the Liberal Party. That's what happens when you build a cabinet out of 29-year-old perpetual students. Chagger has been a Liberal activist since she was 13, dabbling in community volunteerism, including a non-profit theatre company. That's all great; and perhaps it's enough to be an MP, in which attending every festival and being an ombudsman for needy constituents is the job description. But cabinet is the executive of the government. Trump's packing his cabinet with world-class CEOs and former generals who eat nails for breakfast. Trudeau's got Trump beat if the test is a 50% quota for women, another quota for each race and, soon enough, for each sexual orientation.

When Trudeau announced his cabinet, he said he went for gender quotas, "Because it's 2015." That may have been the temper of the times, at least to the TED Talks set. But it's 2017 now. The European Union is crumbling, Russia is a wild card, America is demanding changes to the world order, on everything from trade deals to NATO. Terrorism is rampant, not just in the Islamic State, but in the streets of Europe, and even America. How is volunteering at a Mexican orphanage preparation for that? How can Trudeau's oboe-player energy minister, Jim Carr, even have a substantive conversation with Trump's energy secretary, Rick Perry, who has spent his life in oil fields?

The Canadian Broadcasting Corporation is thrilled, and like state broadcasters in other countries, it's often a good barometer of the government's thinking. After Trudeau's cabinet shuffle, the CBC quoted a senior Liberal strategist, Peter Donolo, who called Trump's cabinet a "geritocracy," and couldn't wait for Trudeau's young gang to run circles around Trump's old farts:

"The chief [Canadian] interlocutors with the Trump administration are going to be this feisty, ball of fire, four-foot-five woman who is on Putin's no fly list. There's a defence minister who is a turbaned Sikh. An immigration minister who is a Muslim born in Somalia. A French-Canadian trade minister. I think it's great. The contrast is tremendous. I think one is a last gasp of a certain kind of politics and culture and the other one is the future."

It's all there, isn't it? The moral superiority, the implication that Trump is a racist and a sexist, and the certainty that what Canada's cabinet ministers lack in experience or wisdom, they'll make up for in moral preening and condescending lectures.

And if that doesn't work for Rex Tillerson, well, Freeland can always have a good cry on TV.

FIVE

COOLING ON GLOBAL WARMING

Donald Trump and Justin Trudeau don't have much in common, but both men are obsessed by global warming. Yet that's like saying both cops and robbers are obsessed by banks — they're coming at it from opposite sides.

Other than the subject of China, and *The Apprentice*, there are few things Trump likes to tweet about more than global warming — even though it's often just the same joke again and again.

"It snowed over 4 inches this past weekend in New York City. It is still October. So much for Global Warming."

"It's extremely cold in NY & NJ—not good for flood victims. Where is global warming?"

"It's freezing and snowing in New York--we need global warming!"

"It is snowing in Jerusalem and across Lebanon. Global warming!"

"They changed the name from 'global warming' to 'climate

change' after the term global warming just wasn't working (it was too cold)!"

When he's not making "cold enough for ya?" jokes, Trump gets into the science and the politics of it. He compares the bafflegab and deliberate obfuscation used to sell the politics of global warming to the discredited "expert" behind Obamacare, Jonathan Gruber: "Just like Jonathan Gruber viciously lied & called Americans 'stupid' on ObamaCare, many consultants are doing the same on Global Warming." He calls global warming lobbyists "dollar sucking wise guys." Unlike most conservative politicians, he's not afraid of challenging the junk science upon which global warming politics are built: "Obama said in his SOTU that 'global warming is a fact.' Sure, about as factual as 'if you like your healthcare, you can keep it'."

Trump talks about the environmental costs of so-called solutions to global warming, like wind turbines: "Windmills are the greatest threat in the US to both bald and golden eagles. Media claims fictional 'global warming' is worse."

Trump isn't anti-environmentalist; he just knows the difference between a false alarm about harmless, colourless, odourless carbon dioxide — the official enemy of the warmists — and actually cleaning up the land, water and air: "Give me clean, beautiful and healthy air - not the same old climate change (global warming) bullshit! I am tired of hearing this nonsense."

Trump has called global warming "bullshit" three times, and a "hoax" eight times — and that's just on Twitter. He calls it a cash grab, but he also sees the underlying ideology behind it: "Surprise? 1970's global cooling alarmists were pushing same no-growth liberal agenda as today's global warming."

But mainly, Trump just likes mocking those who believe in it: "It is really too bad that the scientists studying GLOBAL WARMING in Antarctica got stuck on their icebreaker because of massive ice and cold."

There are other conservatives who oppose the politics of global warming, too. Some say they accept the science of global warming, but disagree about the right way to deal with it — so they'd oppose carbon taxes.

Others just kick the can down the road, saying the science is in dispute, and more study is needed.

Most conservatives either avoid the question where possible, and when cornered, grudgingly mouth the mantras of global warming: mankind caused it; we're all going to die if we don't do something about it; and that something usually involves taxes and regulations for normal people, and subsidies for special people.

That's not Trump's style — he prefers to be the one guy laughing and heckling, while pointing out that the emperor has no clothes. He surely knows that global warming worriers are unlikely to change their minds. But he also knows that those worriers are a distinct minority of the public, even if they dominate the official chattering classes.

In a major survey on the subject released just a month before the 2016 election, the non-partisan Pew Research Center found that few Americans believe in global warming, and few people care. One Pew chart is called "Minority of U.S. adults see climate scientists' research and understanding in a positive light." According to it, only 33% of adults think climate scientists understand "very well" if climate change is occurring. And that's "climate scientists." David Suzuki is not a climate scientist — he's a fruit fly scientist. Bill Nye the Science Guy is not a climate scientist. Only a third of adults think even the specialists know what they're talking about. Fewer still think climate scientists know what's causing "climate change" — 28%. And only 19% think climate scientists know what to do about it.

Normal people are more skeptical about authority than today's journalists.

Pew found that people don't believe the media's claim that there's a scientific consensus about global warming — the much-touted "97%" urban legend. Only 27% of adults surveyed say they agree that "almost all" scientists say climate change is human-caused.

More people (36%) think the scientists' results were guided more by career advancement than what their actual evidence showed (32%). Twenty-seven per cent said it was a result of the scientists' own political leanings; 26% said it was to promote specific industries — e.g., solar panels or wind turbines.

Pew also found that worrying about global warming was a luxury item — the kind of thing that wealthy elites cared about, or at least said they cared about. Working class Americans — the blue collar voters who went for Trump en masse in the rust belt — don't have the time, or extra cash, for fashion statements like that.

Trump knows what he's doing; he knows the media elites are out of sync with the public; he knows that no one trusts politicians on the subject, and few people trust the scientists. He knows "his people" care more about tax relief and jobs than UN treaties that claim to be able to change the weather.

But he also knows that the whole subject is fake — a hoax, as he calls it. Pew found that only 11% of Americans say they follow global warming news very closely. More Americans refuse to follow it at all — they immediately turn the channel. Nobody cares — except the know-nothing elites who pretend to be experts, but couldn't tell you the difference between CO2 or CH4, and can't explain why the last Ice Age ended thousands of years before the SUV was invented. But they're absolutely certain we have to raise taxes because of it.

If Justin Trudeau were to have answered that Pew survey, he'd be in the top percentile — a total believer, if not quite an understander. And Canada's media have enabled him and supported him, not only with uncritical questions about his own plans, but by witch-hunting any opposition politician (or industry leader) who dares to question the science, economics or environmentalism of global warming politics.

Trudeau could get away with repeating trite cliches about global warming when comparable leaders in his league were saying the same thing — Ontario's Kathleen Wynne, Alberta's Rachel Notley, Barack Obama and the European political elites. Saying and doing the same thing as everyone else makes it non-newsworthy. But that's about to change. Trump isn't just going to break away from the elite consensus on global warming. He's going to mock it and ridicule it; he's going to pit himself against it, because he knows the same math that Pew knows: most Americans don't care, and if they do, they're with him.

But unlike other areas of policy — such as on Cuba or Iran — Trump isn't likely to try to get Trudeau to change course, because Trump knows that Trudeau's obsession with global warming doesn't hurt anyone except Canada. And when it comes to luring jobs back to the U.S., an uncompetitive business environment in Canada actually helps him, especially when it comes to repatriating energy-intensive factories, like auto assembly plants. That was precisely the fear Trump expressed back in 2013, after Obama made a key global warming speech. Trump worried that China would just laugh and scoop up more business, while Obama was busy impressing the press gallery know-nothings: "China loved Obama's climate change speech yesterday. They laughed! It hastens their takeover of us as the leading world economy."

Now the roles have switched: Trudeau's the one preening for the cameras, while Trump couldn't be more explicit that his priority is to bring factories back to the U.S. heartland. That pressure so far has been focused on Mexico and China, Trump's two perennial whipping boys; he hasn't spent a lot of time on Canada (and there's plenty of reasons for Canadians to hope he never does). But even if Trump doesn't try to pull factories to relocate from Canada to the U.S., Trudeau is happy to provide plenty of push.

Even before Trudeau was elected Prime Minister — when Stephen Harper was standing between Canadians and a carbon tax, and even while Obama was doing his best to make U.S. taxes and energy more expensive — there was a constant caravan of factories shutting down in Canada's industrial heartland, many of which were relocated to the U.S. — from food manufacturers like Heinz and Kellogg's, to heavy equipment manufacturers such as John Deere and Caterpillar. Electrolux closed its operation in Quebec and moved to Tennessee. Just a month after Trump was elected, Ontario's Leland Industries said it would open its next plant in the U.S., not Ontario, because of the cost of electricity.

All that was before Trudeau's national carbon tax, and before

Trump's national tax cut. These policies will only accelerate the jobs drain to the south.

But Trudeau doesn't think so. In fact, he says Trump's plans to ignore global warming are extra super good for Canada — because Canada will get all the benefits that only true believers get.

"I know Canada is well positioned to pick up some of the slack and when people finally realize that it's a tremendous business opportunity to lead on climate change, Canada will already have a head start," he told the *Guardian*, a leftist newspaper in the U.K. that prides itself on having the greenest editorial policy of any newspaper. Of course, there is nothing stopping any company in the U.S. from investing in the global warming business right now; it's just that what Trudeau was talking about surely wasn't a true business opportunity, but rather green energy subsidies. The U.S. already had its crony capitalism experiment with so-called "clean energy" under Obama, where $80 billion was earmarked for any politically connected huckster who could put together a flashy PowerPoint presentation. Obama gave a $535 million loan to Solyndra, a solar power company. It took the cash and went bankrupt. An electric car battery company called A123 took $130 million and then went bankrupt. U.S. taxpayers dodged a bullet when electric truck manufacturer Bright Automotive went bankrupt just weeks before getting its $450 million government loan. Ener1, an electric car battery maker, was luckier, getting its $118 million grant before closing shop. Only Tesla keeps limping along — with $4.9 billion in government grants, it was deemed too big to fail.

Are those the kind of "tremendous business opportunities" Trudeau is talking about — "when people finally realize" it?

What possible business opportunity could there be in Canada that there isn't in the U.S., other than ones driven by plain, old corporate welfare? And don't green manufacturers want to be located in a low-cost jurisdiction, just like any other company? When Tesla was scouting out locations for its new "Gigafactory," it specifically ruled out any jurisdiction with a sales tax — which would include Trudeau's plans for Canada. They chose low-tax Nevada. And while Tesla boasts that its factory will be a "net zero" facility powered only by renewables, the plant has opened, but the green energy part has not. Tesla's PR pictures still show an artist's conception of the factory, with a gleaming solar-panelled roof and a nearby wind turbine farm, but neither exist in real life. Whether it's for engineering reasons or cost reasons, it's just a regular factory. No one builds solar panels at factories powered by solar panels; no one builds wind turbines at factories powered by wind turbines. What Trudeau means by "tremendous business opportunities" is that he is willing to shovel Canadian tax subsidies at media-savvy impresarios like Elon Musk, in return for plenty of photo ops. And if they have to Photoshop in pictures of actual solar panels later ... well, that's just politics. It worked well enough for Obama — for about two years.

Trudeau has invested so much of his political effort into global warming and his plans for global warming taxes and regulations, he really doesn't seem able to imagine politics or economics without it. A week after his *Guardian* interview, he was still talking about how investors everywhere will be fleeing Trump's America and pouring money into Canada. "If the United States wants to take a step back from it, quite frankly, I think we should look at that as an extraordinary opportunity for Canada and for

Canadians, an opportunity to draw in investors who are focused on where the profits and the opportunities are going to be 10 years from now, 20 years from now," he said. Perhaps that's a different message — an acknowledgement that whatever Trudeau's hypothetical green companies might look like, they'll lose money for twenty years. It's hard to take seriously the economic predictions of the Prime Minister who famously promised that Canada's budget would "balance itself" — and then turned a balanced budget into a $29 billion deficit in just one year. But even if Trudeau's predictions are correct — that there are futuristic green technologies that he just knows in his bones are worth investing in, and that if investors can just hold off for twenty years, they'll start to get a rate of return — is there a single company he can name that would take that deal?

It's not clear whether Trudeau actually believes his own spin that carbon taxes make Canada a more attractive place for investors who "get it," and that they'll choose Canada over Trump's America. In the same interview where Trudeau was trying to show how much better he is at economic development, he was also saying that Trump really wasn't in charge of U.S. climate change policy — real Americans really were going to continue down Barack Obama's path, the same path he was going: "You know quite frankly at the subnational level in the United States, states, municipalities are already showing that they understand that climate change is real so that the potential for the federal government to ease off on actions is not total."

What does that mean? The greenest of the green states, Washington, had a referendum on a Trudeau-style carbon tax on the same day as the 2016 presidential vote. It should have been a

slam dunk — Washington voters overwhelmingly chose Bernie
Sanders in the Democratic primary; and they voted for Hillary
Clinton over Donald Trump by a 15% margin. But those same
voters sent the carbon tax down in flames, losing 41% to 59%.
When even Hillary Clinton voters think a tax is a bad idea, you've
got a loser.

It's true that the U.S. system allows for different states to
try different things. Despite Trump, some states will continue
to ban fracking; some states will continue to tax themselves into
submission. But the biggest environmental decisions in recent
years have been made in Washington, D.C. — like the EPA's war
against coal, which is about to be called off. Even the U.S. fracking
boom, as important as it has been, was restricted on federal lands,
something that will also change under Trump.

California and other states do have a cap-and-trade scheme
for carbon dioxide. But it's a failure by any possible measure.
The "price" for carbon credits in California has plunged to less
than $13/ton — a fraction of what Trudeau, Notley and Wynne
are forcing Canadians to pay in taxes — because there is no real
market for imaginary rights to use energy. Sometimes, several days
go by when not a single carbon credit is bought — it's not a real
commodity, like soya beans or bushels of wheat, that people really
need. A decade ago, banks around the world were looking to cash
in on carbon trading — Enron style. But as Obama lost control of
the U.S. Congress and the European Union had bigger economic
issues to deal with, those hopes faded. In the past five years, the
"carbon trading desks" at Deutsche Bank, UBS, Barclays, Credit
Suisse and countless others have been downsized or shut down
completely. Without politicians artificially forcing people to buy

carbon credits, it just doesn't happen — it's just another Solyndra. Justin Trudeau wants to get in on the Ponzi scheme after it's all over. It was always built on the greater fool theory: sure, you'd be a sucker to think a carbon credit was worth something, but a bigger sucker was just about to come along, maybe because the government forced him to do it. But Trudeau is happy to make Canada the mark, even after the con has been exposed.

Even on its own terms, California's carbon trading scheme is a failure. In 2012 and 2013, the years the program went into effect, California's greenhouse gas emissions went up, while in the rest of the U.S., emissions went down, largely because of the switch to natural gas, which was made affordable by fracking. California has done the opposite: its environmental paranoia made it shut down a safe, zero-emissions nuclear plant, which had to be made up for by burning fossil fuels — so 61% of the state's electricity now comes from carbon, up from 47%. In other words, all of those subsidized Teslas driving around Silicon Valley are actually powered by coal.

But even if there were such a thing as a "carbon market," and even if it reduced emissions by a percent here or there, it would all be wiped out by a few weeks' worth of new coal-fired power plants in China and India, both of which are in the midst of a great industrial revolution. One has to wonder: for all that effort, all that pain and dislocation, does Justin Trudeau actually believe that his carbon schemes will change the weather? He never quite comes right out and says it; he still tries to sell his taxes as some sort of economic magnet. He never says how many fractions of a degree the planet will be cooled by his plans. "We have to counter climate change. Climate change isn't a debate, it's a reality," he told CKNW radio in Vancouver. If that's the case, Trudeau and Trump live in very different realities.

In one way, though, Trudeau has been vindicated. For years, he claimed that the United States would approve the Keystone XL pipeline, which would run from the oilsands down to Texas, if only Canada were to impose a carbon tax on itself. "If we had had an actual price on carbon, if we had figured out some way of actually demonstrating to our trading partners that we are serious about reducing carbon pollution, Keystone XL would already be approved," he said. No one from the Obama administration ever said that; and the U.S. has never made "carbon" a reason to impose trade barriers on any country, including China, the world's largest emitter. But it was a handy excuse Trudeau gave himself for imposing a carbon tax on Canadians. Ironically, it was only after Trudeau was elected that Obama formally decided to veto the pipeline, after years of delay. The deal was dead, and Hillary Clinton, though she had been sympathetic to the pipeline as secretary of state, made it clear in her presidential campaign that she had come to oppose it.

But now the U.S. is set to approve the Keystone XL pipeline after all. Trump had spoken in support of the pipeline during the campaign. But since his election win, there have been press reports that Trump is looking to approve it on his very first day in office. According to Bloomberg News, Trump's plan could involve scrapping a presidential order made by Lyndon B. Johnson near 50 years ago, which gave the State Department the power to review every cross-border pipeline. Scrapping that rule wouldn't only be the fastest way to get the pipeline built, it would vaporize a whole bureaucracy — and a whole lobbying industry — that grew up around that power.

Incredibly — or completely predictably, depending on how cynical you are — now that the U.S. seems on the verge of approving the pipeline, Trudeau's energy minister is having second thoughts. Trudeau had supported Keystone XL as long as Obama and Clinton had seemed certain to block it. Now that it really might happen, well, Jim Carr says it's not really that important to Canada after all, and the Liberals would prefer to sell oil to Asia. Carr's opinion is revealing, but unimportant — Canada's National Energy Board approved Keystone XL back in 2010, after a full hearing. Then again, the Northern Gateway pipeline received NEB approval, too, but Trudeau vetoed it.

It's unlikely that Justin Trudeau, even on his most petulant days, would dare to tell Donald Trump he was blocking an already-approved oil pipeline to the U.S., in favour of selling that same oil to China. It's hard to know what Trump would do in return, but it would probably involve a wall.

SIX

DO YOU WANT TO BE EXTREMELY VETTED?

With his flare for the dramatic, and his brash New York style, there aren't a lot of things that Donald Trump would never say. But this declaration by Justin Trudeau, made during a campaign stop in Winnipeg in the summer of 2015, would be unthinkable for Trump: "the Liberal Party believes that terrorists should get to keep their Canadian citizenship. Because I do. And I'm willing to take on anyone who disagrees with that. Because the question is, as soon as you make citizenship for some Canadians conditional on good behaviour, you devalue citizenship for everyone. A Canadian is a Canadian is a Canadian."

Trudeau was criticizing a decision by the Conservative government to revoke the Canadian citizenship of convicted terrorists, if they're also citizens of a second country. That's a lot of layers — they have to be convicted of terrorism, not just charged or suspected; and they have to still be a citizen of a foreign land, they wouldn't be rendered stateless. But to Trudeau, letting foreign terrorists keep their Canadian passports, even after committing a terrorist act, is proof of just how valuable that citizenship is.

It's hard enough to believe Trudeau said it, frankly. Trump's DNA would literally prevent him from saying such a thing.

Part of it may come from Trudeau's stated belief that Canada is a "post-national" country — that the concept of citizenship means little more than a driver's licence — although even a driver's licence can be taken away from you for bad behaviour. Part of it can be chalked up to Trudeau's campaign strategy of being the candidate of choice for Muslims — even extremist, sharia-law supporting Muslims, who might sympathize with terrorists.

But it's probably his truly held view, too — like his instincts on Cuba, China and Iran, Trudeau takes a Third Worldist position. He's the opposite of a nativist (someone with a bias for his own country). He's an alienist, to coin a term — the more different someone is, the more Trudeau likes him, as a public demonstration of his open-mindedness. Tolerating someone who is convicted of terrorism is the ultimate proof of his open-mindedness. There's a popular meme circulating the Internet, quoting Trudeau as saying, "if you kill your enemies, they win." There's no proof Trudeau actually said it. But if you took it out of quotation marks, it's an accurate paraphrase of the man's views when it comes to Islamic terrorism.

When a Muslim terrorist went on a rampage on Parliament Hill in 2014 — first murdering Cpl. Nathan Cirillo, a Canadian soldier standing at the National War Memorial, and then storming the Parliamentary buildings in a hail of gunfire — Trudeau made a public statement, as did the other party leaders. It was clearly an act of terrorism; it was done by a Muslim; and if there was any doubt, the RCMP later released a cell phone video recorded by the terrorist immediately before his attack, in which he said that punishing Canada for its role in Afghanistan was his main motivation, and that he was doing it in the name of Allah. But in his remarks that night, Trudeau did not one use the word "terrorism."

Trudeau called the terrorist a "shooter," as if the weapon was the most salient characteristic, rather than the motive. He called the terrorist a "criminal," but would not name the crime. Then Trudeau started to lecture — to lecture Canadians, to scold them and warn them not to "speculate" about the terrorist's motives.

And then Trudeau spoke to those who he regarded as the true victims — Canada's Muslims. "To our friends and fellow citizens in the Muslim community, Canadians know acts such as these, committed in the name of Islam, are an aberration of your faith. Continued, mutual cooperation and respect will help prevent the influence of distorted ideological propaganda posing as religion."

Are those really the people who needed consoling at that moment? Cpl. Cirillo's body was still warm, Parliament itself had been breached, it was a miracle that no one was killed inside, including MPs. But Trudeau's first thoughts were to tell Canadians not to "speculate" about things, and to tell Muslims that he knew this Muslim terrorist wasn't Muslim, at least not a real Muslim — and apparently Trudeau's belief in that wasn't speculation.

On the one-year anniversary of the attack, when all the facts about the Muslim terrorist were revealed — including the full videotape — Trudeau still couldn't bring himself to utter the word "terrorism" in his statement, though he did attend the memorial ceremony, along with Stephen Harper, three days after winning the election. But by the second anniversary, when Trudeau himself was the Prime Minister, no memorial ceremonies were permitted or planned, just a perfunctory press release.

Trudeau skipped any ceremonies marking the 15th anniversary of 9/11. But the next day, he made a PR visit to an Ottawa mosque whose website contains links to jihadist propaganda, including a call for the collapse of western civilization, to be replaced with a Muslim theocracy. That's not even remarkable these days — if a Prime Minister is fine going to a mosque that has been used as a terrorist recruitment centre, some website links probably aren't going to keep him away. But what was so striking about this 9/11 mosque visit was that Trudeau — the politician who flew to Davos to give a speech about what a good feminist he was — participated in a gender-apartheid ceremony. No Muslim women were allowed to be near Trudeau as he toured the place — they were up top in a balcony, craning their necks to see him. "Diversity can be a source of strength, not just a source of weakness," he said. But not diversity when it comes to gender equality. "And as I look at this beautiful room, with the sisters upstairs," he continued, not once mentioning the fact that the "sisters upstairs" had been forced into segregation. Trudeau then tweeted some photos of himself meeting around tables with a group of Muslim men — but with two of Trudeau's female cabinet ministers in tow, including his hyper-feminist environment minister, Catherine McKenna. Both of Trudeau's cabinet ministers — non-Muslims — were wearing hijabs, the Muslim headscarf.

The Muslim mosque didn't have to accept Canadian customs,

but Canadian cabinet ministers had to accept Muslim customs.

Trudeau has never said the words, "if you kill your enemies, they win," but he's said as much in other words.

He's bragged about campaigning in the most extremist mosques in Canada — including Montreal's Assuna Wahhabi mosque, which is funded by Saudi Arabia and has been accused by the U.S. government of being a recruiting centre for terrorists. Even the pro-Muslim CBC did an investigation into the mosque and revealed its extremist teachings, including that the proper punishment for sins like adultery is death. Trudeau didn't care. "My job as MP for Papineau, is to represent citizens of my riding," he told *Maclean's* magazine. "Everyone in that mosque was a Canadian. You can disagree with them and you can be worried about what some people might be preaching, but, for me, it's more important that my message of respect and inclusion … is an approach that I will consistently take." But Trudeau has never taken a message of inclusion into the mosques — not for the women, gays or religious minorities that Islam has historically persecuted. The only message of respect and inclusion that Trudeau takes is for Canadians to submit to Islam — including his own female cabinet ministers. Even Hillary Clinton and Michelle Obama kept their hair uncovered when they visited Saudi Arabia. Trudeau's staff won't even do so in the capital city of Canada.

In his very first phone call with Barack Obama after Trudeau's election — a quick congratulatory call from Obama, before Trudeau was even sworn in officially — Trudeau blurted out his plans to withdraw Canada's CF-18 jets from the U.S.-led coalition that was fighting the Islamic State. Of all the issues between Canada and the U.S., to focus on that as the highest priority; to break diplomatic protocol, to turn a friendly, informal call into an ultimatum and then to tell reporters about it — that was a shock to the Americans, especially to the Obama administration, which had seen Trudeau as a fellow traveller and had shared campaign staff with the Liberals. The U.S. ambassador to Canada tried to respond in kind, going on an unprecedented PR tour to try to convince the Liberals to keep the six Canadian jets in the coalition. Those six jets did important work, flying hundreds of sorties. But in the grand scheme of things, they weren't militarily essential — the U.S. had many times more aircraft in the region, either at military bases or on aircraft carriers. It was the symbolism of Canada's involvement — to prove that the anti-ISIS coalition was more than just the U.S. If Obama couldn't even convince Canada, America's closest ally, to keep six planes in the fight, why should other countries stick around, either? But Trudeau was adamant.

Like Trudeau, Barack Obama has always been loath to use the word "terrorism," and the phrase "Muslim terrorism" never crossed his lips. He's the president who flew to Cairo to introduce himself to the Muslim world by emphasizing his middle name, Hussein, and said that "the sweetest sound I know is the Muslim call to prayer." If that guy thinks you're too soft on Muslim terrorism, you're probably too soft on Muslim terrorism.

Obama never truly tried to eradicate the Islamic State; even after a decade of military cuts, the Pentagon still had the men and machines to wipe out the rag-tag terrorist enclave in Syria and Iraq in a matter of weeks, if it wanted to. But Obama was trapped by his own 2012 campaign promises to completely withdraw American troops from the region. Sending them back in would have been tantamount to an admission that his strategy was wrong all along.

But Donald Trump couldn't be more hawkish when it comes to ISIS. Trump is more of an isolationist than Obama; he's questioned the Bush-Obama legacy of attempted nation-building in the Middle East. Unlike the neo-cons, Trump repeatedly calls the 2003 invasion of Iraq a disaster. But destroying ISIS is so important to him, his campaign's foreign policy is actually called, "Foreign Policy and Defeating ISIS":

"Pursue aggressive joint and coalition military operations to crush and destroy ISIS, international cooperation to cutoff their funding, expand intelligence sharing, and cyberwarfare to disrupt and disable their propaganda and recruiting.

"Defeat the ideology of radical Islamic terrorism just as we won the Cold War."

There's not a lot of wiggle room there. What will Trudeau say when Trump inevitably calls on Canada to "crush and destroy" ISIS as part of a coalition? How could Canada's contribution to such a serious effort possibly be any less than what Canada had done with Obama's half-hearted approach?

When Barack Obama and Hillary Clinton came up with an ill-conceived scheme to depose Libyan leader Moammar Gadhafi, there wasn't a conceivable Canadian national interest at stake. Gadhafi had undergone a remarkable transformation — rejecting terrorism and paying billions in reparations to victims of the 1988 Libyan bombing of a Pan-Am flight over Lockerbie, Scotland. He gave up his chemical weapons and abandoned Libya's plans for nuclear weapons. It was such a dramatic change of course that Canada's Prime Minister at the time, Paul Martin, flew to Libya to praise the man and renew trade ties. Many western leaders did.

Gadhafi was still a dictator, to be sure. But he had seen what happened to Iraq and made the enlightened decision to cast his lot with the winners. And however cruel or quirky he was, he was all that was holding back Islamic terrorism in his country.

But when Obama and Clinton wanted regime change, and wanted the political cover of doing so with an allied coalition, Harper agreed. It wasn't just a token force — seven CF-18s, eight other planes and two warships. In fact, a Canadian general led the NATO forces. Harper put the military mission to a debate and a vote in Parliament, where it passed unanimously. Luckily, there were no Canadian casualties. But the real reason Canada chose a war with no real purpose, no precise definition of victory and no Canadian connection, was because Canada is America's closest and most loyal ally. And sometimes — including in fool's errands, like a war in Libya — you help out a friend, even when that friend is misguided. That's a pessimistic definition of the word "allies," but it's part of it.

Who knows what Harper got in return. Maybe a pass on a more dangerous U.S.-led military mission; maybe a private promise not to ramp-up protectionist measures against Canadian imports. Maybe even a pledge that Obama would still consider approving the Keystone XL pipeline, or at least delay killing it. Given that Obama announced his veto of that project shortly after Trudeau stiffed him on CF-18s for the ISIS mission, that's a real possibility. But the point is, when the president of the United States asks Canada for something, even something that we would normally not do, that request can't be denied lightly.

What will Canada do when Trump asks for those jets back? Unlike the Libyan invasion — which soon turned that stable country into a failed state, overrun with Islamic terrorists —

Trump's plan is clearly defined and arguably in Canada's interests. ISIS is at war with Canada, directly, when it can be, and indirectly, as a source of inspiration to lone wolf terrorists, like the one who attacked Parliament in 2014. And the mere existence of the Islamic State as a geographic safe haven for terrorists is a major security risk for Canada — Canadian Muslims travel there, become deeply indoctrinated in the terrorist philosophy and receive military-style training. So far, no Canadian terrorists have returned to Canada to commit attacks, but recent attacks in Europe suggest it's only a matter of time. Destroying ISIS and obliterating its actual geographic footprint wouldn't just be a material setback for Islamic terrorism, it would be an enormous symbolic defeat, puncturing the messianic confidence that is part of its propaganda. The Islamic State really wants to set up an Islamic state. Trump wants to take that away, and he wants our help. Is Trudeau really going to refuse?

Barack Obama won the Nobel Peace Prize and proceeded to attacked seven countries during his term in office. Trump's foreign policy explicitly swears off regime change and nation-building. Other than defeating ISIS, the rest of his foreign policy is actually domestic policy: screening out Muslim extremists, or what Trump calls "extreme vetting." Trump shocked the political campaign when he first suggested he would institute a ban on Muslim travel to the U.S. But in a major speech on the subject, he outlined in practical terms what he meant:

"In the Cold War, we had an ideological screening test. The time is overdue to develop a new screening test for the threats we face today. I call it extreme vetting. Any who have hostile attitudes towards our country or its principles or who believe that sharia law should supplant American law. Those who do not believe in our constitution or who support bigotry and hatred will not be admitted."

Trump's policies also emphasize security screening to weed out terrorists. But many terrorists are not detectable in advance — they don't have previous criminal records for terrorism offences. What's new in Trump's plan is the idea of screening people for values, to weed out those who would be more likely to become terrorists, based on their ideology.

Trump's official campaign platform didn't call for a ban on Muslims, per se; it called for a temporary suspension of immigration from terrorist-infested countries — that all happen to be Muslim: "Suspend, on a temporary basis, immigration from some of the most dangerous and volatile regions of the world that have a history of exporting terrorism." And Trump's last policy point is the most politically incorrect of all: "Establish a Commission on Radical Islam to identify and explain to the American public the core convictions and beliefs of Radical Islam, to identify the warning signs of radicalization, and to expose the networks in our society that support radicalization."

What a contrast with Barack Obama and Hillary Clinton, who actively courted the Muslim Brotherhood — a radical Islamic political affiliation that includes the terrorist group Hamas. But note again, Trump isn't merely focusing on the symptoms of terrorism — he's focusing on the causes, and he's identified that cause as Islam itself. It's like the difference between a metal detector at an airport, which only scans for metallic weapons, and actually interviewing people before they get on the plane, to see if they're a possible threat. That's the kind of extreme vetting that is done at Israel's international airport, out of necessity. Trump is saying that necessity has come to America and he's not going to be politically correct about it.

Perhaps even more than Trump's pledge to build a wall along the Mexican border, his Muslim vetting plan elicited the most apoplectic reaction from the media and political establishment. That's because it's Trump's specialty: calling out the emperor's new clothes, saying what everyone else knows, but is afraid to mention out of good manners. Trump's worst personal trait — his rudeness — is actually his best personal trait — honesty. Fear of radical Islam is legitimate, not just in America itself, but as Americans watch the Islamification of Europe, through mass, unvetted migration. The political classes have demonized that fear, giving it an epithet, "Islamophobia," literally meaning "fear of Islam." No liberal dared to be seen as Islamophobic, for fear of not being seen as progressive enough; no conservative dared to, for fear of being labelled a racist. Trump doesn't care about name-calling — he just name-calls right back. Calling out the threat to America by name — radical Islam — and comparing it to past ideological threats, like Communism and Nazism, is a conversation that no one in America wanted to have, except the voters.

Contrast that to Justin Trudeau, who could properly be called an Islamophile. No Muslim mosque is too extreme for him to visit; no Muslim conference too radical for him to speak at. He prays Muslim prayers, publishes photos of his mother and wife wearing veils and puts his female cabinet ministers in them, too. His mouth literally cannot form the words "radical Islam" — as his reflexive reaction to the Muslim terrorist attack on Parliament Hill showed. Even when a Muslim terrorist said he committed terrorism in the name of Islam, Trudeau wouldn't accept it, calling it "propaganda" and an "aberration." That's wilful blindness to Trump.

Like Trudeau is in Canada, Trump is the most liberal president ever when it comes to gay rights. He famously held up a rainbow-coloured flag during a campaign rally, with the words "LGBT for Trump," and "Gays for Trump" placards could be seen at many of his rallies. Entire battalions of proudly gay Trump supporters fought campaign battles on Twitter and Facebook, especially after the Muslim terrorist attack on a gay nightclub in Orlando, Florida, that killed 49 and left 53 injured. In campaign speeches, Trump repeatedly attacked the Muslim extremist practice of killing gays and mentioned it specifically in his major immigration speech.

Trudeau is a gay-friendly Prime Minister, too — if there's a gay pride parade somewhere in Canada, you'll be sure to see Trudeau there, in his bright pink shirt and bead necklaces. But it's just the costume of the day for him; he'll be at the mosque the next day, wearing a desert-style abaya smock, and any women in his entourage will be covered from head to toe.

None of that would likely matter to Trump — how a Canadian Prime Minister campaigns in Canada isn't something he'd care about. But Trudeau has decided that part of his campaigning in Canada is to use Trump as a cautionary tale. Trudeau's real political base is the media; and Canadian journalists, like those in the U.S., didn't even try to restrain their partisan support for Hillary Clinton before the election, or their rage against Trump and his supporters after it. But they're just pundits. Trudeau is our head of government.

A week before Trump's inauguration, Trudeau was asked about his relations with the incoming president. "Canadians expect their government to have a constructive working relationship with the incoming American administration, and that's exactly what we're going to do," he said. That's the right answer — the same as Stephen Harper must have said when his ideological and stylistic opposite, Barack Obama, was elected in 2008. But Trudeau couldn't just leave it at that. He was at a campaign-style town hall, trying to shore up his popularity after a particularly bad month of scandals. So he reached for the sure-fire winner, at least in Liberal circles: bash Trump.

"Canada is a separate country from the United States and there are things that we hold dear that the Americans haven't prioritized," he added. "And I'm never going to shy away from standing up for what I believe in — whether it's proclaiming loudly to the world that I am a feminist, whether it's understanding that immigration is a source of strength for us and Muslim Canadians are an essential part of the success of our country today and into the future."

That may be in Trudeau's personal interest to say — women and Muslims were an important part of his electoral coalition. But how is that in Canada's interest for Trudeau to say, in public, a week before the U.S. inauguration, before he's even had a meeting with Trump? And even if Trudeau were right and Trump was wrong, what does that have to do with the Canada-U.S. relationship?

Feminism is not a Canada-U.S. issue. There is no systemic mistreatment of women in America. Trudeau likes to present himself as a white knight coming in to protect damsels in distress. But on what possible bilateral issue with the United States is that relevant? Softwood lumber? The war on ISIS? A "Buy American" policy for U.S. procurement? Pipeline politics? None of these, of course. It's Trudeau rehashing his comments from October 2016, when he said that, unlike Trump, he is "someone who has stood thoroughly and strongly all my life around issues of sexual harassment, standing against violence against women." It's just a personal attack. Trump knows how to handle those — make a personal attack right back. It's one of the reasons why he loves Twitter so much. Trump's going to make Trudeau even more famous one day.

But to bundle a personal innuendo against Trump with the real issue of Muslim migration is playing with fire. Trump was clear: he's going to step-up security screenings; he's going to pause migration from Muslim countries; he's going to test newcomers for adherence to American values; and he's going to have a commission studying radical Islam. None of that has anything to do with Canada. But for some reason, Justin Trudeau thinks it does — at least, enough to weld it to an answer, when asked about Canada-U.S. relations.

The truth is, Canada's lax approach to Muslim immigration is a U.S. issue, and has been for a long time, even before 9/11. Ahmed Ressam, the so-called "Millennium Bomber," was an Al Qaeda terrorist from Algeria, who trained in Afghanistan and planned to detonate a bomb hidden in a suitcase in a passenger waiting area at the Los Angeles airport. Trouble is, Ressam was based in Montreal, and he crossed into the U.S. from British Columbia. Ressam had actually been caught by police in Canada several times. When he first landed in Canada, immigration officials arrested him for using a fake passport. But he was allowed to stay. He made a refugee application, which was rejected, as was the appeal — but still he was allowed to stay. He went back and forth to Afghanistan. In Canada, he was arrested four more times for petty crimes, but still he was allowed to stay. Nearly five years of dealing with Keystone Cops didn't stop him. Only an alert U.S. border guard did — likely saving dozens of lives.

Since then, Canada has admitted close to one million more Muslim migrants, and the terrorist plots haven't stopped. Not just in Canada, but also using Canada as a jumping-off point to the U.S.: the 2013 Via Rail plot — foiled by Canadian police — targeted a passenger train going from Toronto to New York City.

Canada isn't just a destination for Muslim terrorists; it's a source of them. According to Canada's Public Safety Department, 180 Canadians have gone overseas to join terrorist groups and 60 of those have come back to Canada and are now walking the streets. But that report was prepared before Trudeau rushed in more than 25,000 Syrian migrants, from a country with few reliable records, countless competing terrorist and militant groups, and few language and cultural skills. The sheer haste of it meant that normal background checks were impossible. The Canadian government didn't even have enough Arabic speakers to meaningfully interview the people being hoovered up by the thousands, just to comply with Trudeau's artificial deadline.

The Islamic State had publicly boasted, in advance, that it intended to embed its terrorists in the waves of Muslim migrants that were descending on Europe. And indeed it did — fake "refugees" were implicated in recent terrorist attacks on the Bataclan club in Paris, a wine bar in Ansbach, Germany, and the horrific truck-ramming attack on a Christmas market in Berlin, just to name a few.

Each attack in Europe — and those in America — caused a new wave of debate over immigration and security. But not in Canada. Trudeau was adamant that if anything, the answer to Muslim terrorism was more Muslim immigration, not less. In a December 2015 interview on Global News, Trudeau was asked by reporter Dawna Friesen, "If God forbid there was an attack on Canada like the one in Paris would that change the equation for you?" Here's Trudeau's full answer: "Obviously, we are working very hard to both insure that Canadian safety, but also not to give in to the narrative that ISIS wants.

"I mean, if they are posting beheadings on the internet and using advanced videos as recruiting tools, one of things that they need, they need people to be terrorized by terror, they need people to be afraid, people need to be polarized, and that what they are trying to do.

"They would love for us to suddenly be afraid, be more afraid and close in and create walls because that makes it easier for them to achieve their goals. We have to be courageous and confident while we protect Canadians."

A shorter answer would have been "no." But the longer answer is illuminating; it really is a version of the apocryphal quote, "if you kill your enemies, they win." Trudeau's bizarre thesis is that by showing Muslims that Canada lets in thousands of Muslim migrants, that will embarrass ISIS and somehow stop the terrorist threat. There seems to be a pretty big logical leap in there, but the answer is clear: Trudeau says that even if Muslim terrorists come into Canada through his Muslim refugee rush, he's not going to stop the Muslim refugee rush.

That sounds like it should be ISIS's plan, not Canada's.

❖

Trudeau had a few months to practice his answers before appearing on CBS's flagship show, *60 Minutes*.

Trudeau knew he had to have a better answer on screening out terrorist threats. So he just made one up: the preposterous suggestion that Canada had brought in 25,000 Syrian migrants in less than two months — 1,000 Syrian migrants per business day — and that they were screened in anything more than a perfunctory way: "We were able to actually go and pick and choose and screen and bring over the people we chose. And that gives us a much greater level of control and attention over who's actually going to come in." It wasn't true; Canada did not "go and pick and choose" which migrants came to Canada; Canada's foreign ministry didn't have diplomatic staff in Syria at all — the embassy was closed and Syrian affairs are run out of Lebanon. Canada didn't do the picking; that was outsourced to the United Nations and to other agencies in Lebanon, Jordan and Turkey, which are under the control of foreign governments. Polls showed that even liberal Canadians, who had been open to Syrian migrants during the campaign, opposed Trudeau's rush, primarily because of the lack of vetting. And the government refuses to release even the short checklist-style questionnaire Syrian migrants had to fill out. The government's first response was that the questionnaire didn't exist, then it asked for a 10-month delay in releasing it, only to finally declare that national security meant it couldn't be revealed to the Canadian public. Twenty-five thousand Syrian strangers could learn about our paper-thin background checks. But not concerned Canadian citizens.

Even *60 Minutes* was skeptical; perhaps because reporter Lara Logan herself became a victim of Muslim violence while reporting from Cairo: "Are you saying there's no risk? Or do you acknowledge that there is still a risk?" she asked.

Trudeau said it's a risk, but he's fine with that: "Every time, every time a tourist or an immigrant or a refugee shows up in another country there's a security risk. And, I am more than comfortable that doing what we've done, accepting in 25,000 Syrian refugees does right by both the safety of Canadians and by the values that define us as a nation."

Logan pressed him one more time: "Would you be just as comfortable if there was a terrorist attack carried out by someone who came through as a refugee?" Trudeau answered, "ultimately, being open and respectful towards each other is much more powerful as a way to diffuse hatred and anger than, you know, layering on, you know, big walls and oppressive policies."

The Trudeau interview aired on CBS on March 6, 2016, when Trump was the unquestionable Republican front-runner. The party's default candidate, Jeb Bush, had withdrawn in February and Trump had just scooped up seven of the eleven states on Super Tuesday. It wasn't quite over yet, but the Trump Train had left the station. Trudeau knew that; he was in a foreign country, in its election year, in the midst of a lively primary and he chose not only to promote Canada's policies, but to go out of his way to disparage Trump's "wall" proposal and other "oppressive" policies.

But put aside the insult and look at the answer on its face: Justin Trudeau said that "being open and respectful" really is the way to beat Muslim terrorists. That's the only reasonable explanation of his answer to Logan's question.

It's not just that Trudeau thinks that if you kill you enemies, they win.

Trudeau believes that if they kill you, you win.

Trudeau is willing to sacrifice some Canadians on the altar of his Islamophilia and political correctness. It probably won't be him, with his VIP security detail and his bulletproof limousine. But he's fine with it, at least enough not to change course.

In 2016, the U.K. voted to leave the European Union, in large part because of immigration issues. Two of Trump's top campaign pledges — the Mexican border wall and extreme vetting of Muslims — helped propel him to an upset victory. Anti-migrant candidates are set to win elections in France, the Netherlands and possibly even Germany. And yet Trudeau insists that even if his Syrian scheme kills people, he won't blink.

That's an issue for Canadians to deal with. But Trudeau seems to want to make it an issue for Americans — he won't shut up about it, whether he's at a Canadian town hall meeting or on an American talk show. He really wants to lecture Donald Trump, and scold him. He'll probably lose that argument. But the other 36 million of us will likely pay the price, the least of which would be long line-ups at the border.

SEVEN

WHAT WOULD SOROS DO?

Donald Trump beat Hillary Clinton in the election, and he's in the process of beating her allies in the mainstream media. But there's another, somewhat hidden hand that has been fighting against Trump, which he has yet to take on, at least publicly. That's George Soros, the Hungarian-born billionaire who has long been the richest donor to Democratic causes in the U.S. — and an even bigger financier of left-wing street activism around the world.

Soros has had a colourful career as a financier, making a name for himself as the banker who bet billions against the British pound in 1992 — and crashed the currency. He pushed millions of Brits into poverty, but he made an estimate $1 billion off the deal himself.

This is a man who casts himself as a progressive champion of the underdog.

Soros has been a major donor to Democratic campaigns, spending tens of millions of dollars in a vain attempt to defeat

George W. Bush in 2004, telling the *Washington Post* that beating the Republican was "the central focus of my life." That failed, but Soros also spent tens of millions of dollars setting up countless cookie-cutter "non-partisan" political action groups around America, with vague names like Open Society Foundations, Center for American Progress (CAP) and Americans Coming Together. Some of those groups were shut down for campaign-spending violations; others remain active to this day. CAP, for example, was the political home of John Podesta, who became Hillary Clinton's campaign chairman. Not only did CAP host a gala event for Trudeau during his first trip to Washington as Prime Minister, it also worked with Trudeau's own version of CAP, a non-profit political action group called Canada2020.

Those are the more respectable recipients of Soros's banking profits. Soros specializes in dirtier work, including political action that's done on the streets — sometimes through violence.

In America, that's taken the form of Black Lives Matter, the race-based pressure group that has fomented riots from Ferguson, Missouri, to Milwaukee, Wisconsin, and inspired a wave of anti-police violence. The violence was actually what got Soros excited; in an internal Soros memo released by Wikileaks, Open Society staff wrote this about the Baltimore riots: "While many lamented the damage done, the overwhelming sentiment is that the uprising has catalyzed a paradigm shift in Baltimore that offers opportunities for major justice reforms." So they cut them a $650,000 cheque — crime does pay, when it has a political goal.

Soros has been doing this for years. Last time, it was Occupy Wall Street, the anti-capitalist street gangs famous for squatting in city parks around the U.S. and even in Canadian cities. If Soros doesn't fund a group directly, odds are he funds a middleman who does. Soros has given millions of dollars to the Tides Foundation of San Francisco, which specializes in "donor advised giving" — a sanitized phrase meaning that Soros gets the charitable tax receipt and Tides takes a commission, but the money is essentially laundered. There's no disclosure of what entity receives the money in the end.

It's a great way for U.S. billionaires to muck around in different countries, which Soros likes to do. In 2015 alone, the Tides Foundation made nearly 150 different grants to Canadian political pressure groups, mainly fighting against Canada's oilsands. Aboriginal pressure groups, environmental lawyers and even street protesters like Greenpeace and the Council of Canadians took money from Soros's middleman, Tides. For example, the year before the Canadian federal election, Tides pumped nearly $80,000 into Leadnow, a pro-Trudeau Canadian campaign group that was instrumental in electing Liberal MPs in B.C., on a promise of fighting the oilsands.

That's how Soros fights in Canada and the U.S. The Soros Wikileaks show that he's obsessed with promoting Muslim immigration to the west — and is spending millions of his own dollars forcing Muslim migrants into Europe, by funding political activists and lawyers to batter through any democratic opposition. Soros doesn't hide his goals — he wants to replace the democratically elected leaders in places like Israel, Hungary and elsewhere who get in his way. He has funded successful street revolutions everywhere from Serbia to Georgia. It's what he does.

But money can't buy everything; in fact, Soros's tactics may have backfired in the 2016 election. Trump didn't try to appease

Black Lives Matter. It was a shocking spectacle when a major
Trump rally in Chicago was shut down by Black Lives Matter-
style street thugs, who infiltrated the event, fighting with Trump
supporters and even rioting against the police outside. When
extremists with the Soros-funded group La Raza protested Trump
rallies by blocking highways and flying Mexican flags, it surely
revved up the hard-left. But it shocked middle America — the
very people Trump was targeting. From that moment forward,
Trump made a point of taking photos with police and other law
enforcement personnel at every stop — signalling that the era
of street violence would end under his presidency. To left-wing
activists, the sight of a Mexican flag waving in the streets of
America was very exciting; but for every vote it recruited against
Trump in California, it surely got him five elsewhere, and turned
his promise of building a wall into a sure-fire applause line at
rallies.

Soros and Tides, and other American billionaires, fund dozens
of Canadian lobby groups, including many that registered in the
2015 federal election as what Elections Canada calls "Third Party
Campaigns" — almost all of which campaigned against Stephen
Harper's Conservatives. It's technically illegal for U.S. donors like
Soros to contribute to a Canadian election, but Elections Canada
doesn't have the resources, or the political interest, to audit more
than one hundred groups. And besides, a U.S.-funded lobby
group that paid for its equipment, office and staff with American
money could simply declare that its actual Canadian campaign
expenditures were funded solely by its Canadian donors and that
the American money just bought the building and equipment.

Those hundred-plus Third Parties Campaigns are just the ones that registered and complied with election laws. But others, like the hyper-partisan David Suzuki Foundation, simply refused to file. It's a gamble, but it's probably a smart one. They're taking the position that what they say — when they attack Stephen Harper, or oppose a pipeline — isn't campaigning, and therefore they can spend their money how they like. And who's going to complain — Justin Trudeau?

This cross-border murky funding model is new to most Canadians, but it's old hat to Gerald Butts, who cultivated foreign donors when he ran the Canadian branch of the anti-oil World Wildlife Fund. He's completely comfortable with foreign billionaires and complex financing structures. It's no surprise that when Trudeau went to Davos, he spent some private time with Soros. What was surprising is that Trudeau tweeted a picture of the two of them in an intimate conversation. Normally politicians don't advertise when they meet with foreign billionaires who are known to bankroll campaigns. But again, who's going to investigate — the ethics commissioner?

Who knows what the billionaire and the politician talked about, and whether or not a generous gift was made to one of Trudeau's Canadian street teams, like Leadnow or Canada2020. But several months later, Trudeau announced that the Canadian government was teaming up with Soros and the United Nations, to promote Muslim migration to the west, including a propaganda project to "provide a vehicle that mobilizes citizens in direct support of refugees and encourages a broader political debate that is supportive of refugee protection."

Soros moves fast; three months later, the Canadian government held an international conference to promote Muslim migration to the west. Not only were senior Soros staff helping to run the government event, but an additional name popped up in the official Canadian press release: Frank Giustra. Giustra was a hot potato in the U.S. presidential election because he pledged an eye-popping US$100 million donation to one of the Clinton family foundations, the money machine that made Bill and Hillary filthy rich, while serving as a back door to the U.S. State Department. According to the *Washington Post*, not only did Giustra pledge the nine-figure sum, he let Bill Clinton use his private jet at will — more than 25 flights. Must be nice.

But billionaires, even generous ones, don't usually give something for nothing. Giustra was one of the stars of the best-selling book, *Clinton Cash*, written by Peter Schweizer, and a documentary by the same name. Here's just one curious fact Schweizer unearthed: Giustra had dinner with the Clintons one night in 2010; the next night, the Clintons met with the president of Colombia. A short time later, a company in which Giustra had a stake, "acquired the right to cut timber in a biologically diverse forest on the pristine Colombian shoreline," and another was granted oil drilling rights.

That was chicken feed compared to Giustra's next deal with the Clintons. In 2005, Giustra and Bill Clinton jetted to Kazakhstan to dine with the country's dictator. Days later, Giustra's mining company acquired a stake in three government-run uranium mines, as well as some uranium mines that the Kazakhs controlled in the U.S.

After a US$3.5 billion merger, the Russian nuclear agency, Rosatom, bought out Giustra. But the sale of so much of the world's uranium resources — including in America — required the approval of the U.S. State Department.

Luckily for Giustra, the secretary of state by then was none other than Hillary Clinton herself — so she approved the transfer of the company, which controlled 20% of American uranium production, to Russian ownership.

Giustra denies any wrongdoing; and the Clintons claim that a $500,000 speech Bill gave in Russia had nothing to do with the sale. But the Clinton campaign seemed to acknowledge there was a problem, when it promised mid-campaign that Clinton foundations would stop accepting foreign funds if Hillary became president.

The fact that billionaire Clinton donors have so easily transferred their affections to Justin Trudeau should be of concern to Canadians. First there was the U.K. Brexit referendum, then the Trump win and before the year is out, conservative nationalists may well have ousted Soros-friendly governments in France, Germany, Holland and elsewhere. With three years to go before he faces the electorate again, Trudeau seems to have become Soros's new toy — and the puppet of other Clinton donors, too.

Muslim migration is high on the Soros-Giustra agenda; that may explain why Trudeau has announced that Canada's immigration levels will rise even higher next year, despite polls showing that only a microscopic 8% of Canadians support higher levels. What George Soros wants, George Soros gets. One of Soros's obsessions is with liberalizing voting laws, such as suing to repeal voter ID requirements. That, too, may explain Trudeau's inexplicable infatuation with throwing out Canada's first-past-the-post electoral system, in favour of an ill-defined replacement for which there is no palpable demand. These are Canadian problems, and they go to our national sovereignty, political transparency and the unfortunate Liberal tendency towards financial corruption.

But there is an obvious Canada-U.S. relations aspect to all this, too: George Soros, more than any other American, is the leader of the opposition to Donald Trump. He has no position in Congress, and never will — he's 86 years old. But unlike the Clintons, he's not exhausted; he doesn't care if he's demonized in the media. He knows that real power comes from money — maybe not enough to win the election, but enough to agitate, harass and disrupt. The Soros-backed riot at the Chicago Trump rally backfired. But getting good press is no longer the goal — anti-democratic action is the next move, stirring up conflict and division, muddying the waters and stepping on any good news stories Trump might otherwise earn. He's playing dirty — but that's Soros's specialty.

Clinton herself went into a reclusive funk after she lost; but after a few days of regrouping, far-left street teams of professional protesters rampaged through leftist hotspots, like Portland, Oregon. They not only rioted, Black Lives Matter-style, they threatened any media who dared to videotape them. They even threatened other protesters with "Don't snitch, ever" leaflets — demanding that no cell-phone videos be filmed of the rioters. These weren't organic, spontaneous riots — according to Portland media, 60% of the rioters were from out of state — it was a planned, orchestrated event. Soros rarely takes responsibility for actual violence and it would have been legally dangerous for him to do so in Portland. But two weeks after the election, he announced a US$10 million grant to combat "incendiary rhetoric" from Trump and his supporters. That $10 million will be spent on "community groups and civil rights organizations," to be named later — suggesting that Black Lives Matter and La Raza could be recipients. That's a lot of walking-around money for professional protesters, some of whom are known to charge up to $1,500 a day to protest, Chicago- or Portland-style. That could come as soon as the inauguration, where Soros-backed pressure groups are organizing a week-long series of street demonstrations.

Soros has taken it upon himself to be America's leading anti-Trump gadfly — not even giving Trump the courtesy of a moment's peace for his ceremonial swearing-in. Soros is Trump's problem to deal with — Soros is an American, and any protests in America are for Trump to worry about. But Trudeau is importing Soros, making him a financier, partner and advisor, especially on the core issues for the Trump administration. Trudeau will face enough challenges building a personal relationship with Trump — why is he bringing along the Republicans' public enemy number one, with all his baggage, too?

Of course, it's not just Soros. It's the whole Democratic machine. They all went north to colonize Trudeau's Liberal Party. Jennifer O'Malley Dillon, Obama's assistant campaign manager, was the unofficial ambassador from Obama to Trudeau. Her job was simple: teach him how to defeat a sitting Conservative Prime Minister, Stephen Harper. Her U.S.-based team got in on it, but were clever enough not to tweet about their role publicly, until after the vote was over. George Soros would have approved.

The great David Axelrod, master strategist of Obama's 2008 breakthrough, joined in, too. And Mitch Stewart, Obama's battleground states director, was brought in, as well. It's surprising that the whole campaign wasn't just run out of Washington, or Chicago.

No wonder the Trudeau team wanted to pay it forward. In January 2016, just a week before Trudeau would meet Soros in Davos, Trudeau's team met with the Center for American Progress and offered to return the favour. A memo, revealed by Wikileaks, was sent to Hillary Clinton's campaign chairman and spokesman, letting them know that CAP was "planning a big party in DC" for Trudeau. "And wondered what they might do to help" the campaign.

Gerald Butts, Trudeau's best friend and principal secretary, was his go-between with Soros's front groups. And the same Gerald Butts is reportedly taking meetings at Trump Tower with Trump's transition team. It will be interesting to see how long he'll be able to ride two horses.

EIGHT

THE BLUE-COLLAR
BILLIONAIRE

Can either Donald Trump or Justin Trudeau claim to be a politician who cares about the middle class? How about the working class — blue-collar workers, tradesmen, people who didn't go to college, and if they did, it wasn't to get a degree in feminist studies or interpretive dance?

Can either of them actually claim to be for the forgotten man?

Trump and Trudeau were each born to wealthy families; each love the media spotlight; and each were household names before they were elected as head of government. But apart from that, they couldn't be more different.

Trudeau is the heir of an heir — the second generation of a family to be born into great wealth. And for the first 37 years of his life, he just played around.

He dabbled at school, but lost interest, quitting before finishing a degree in environmentalism. He taught as a substitute teacher for a while, but that didn't keep his attention, either. With low ambitions, a multi-million dollar trust fund, a famous name and good looks, there really was no need to work. So he travelled the world, sowing his wild oats, before finally settling down in middle age.

Trump was born a millionaire's son, too. But he could hardly wait to get to work. He started at his father's real estate company while he was earning an MBA at the Wharton School of Business. He was running the company by age 25, and the rest is history — the real estate, the TV shows, the beauty pageants. Trump claims his personal wealth is $9 billion; Forbes and Fortune magazine put the number at half that. But it's undoubtable that he's the wealthiest president in history.

Trudeau has been less open about his business affairs — mainly because they're still managed by the trust set up by his father. Trudeau likely doesn't know the full value of his wealth, and he still doesn't have full control of it. It's surely in the tens of millions of dollars, not the billions. But it's been enough to cultivate a certain taste and a familiarity with luxury. And what his own trust fund hasn't paid for, his well-heeled friends were only happy to. Trudeau is a millionaire who lives like a billionaire.

That was a private matter until he became an MP. But daily responsibilities just weren't something he was accustomed to. He regularly skipped out of Parliamentary work, for unexplained reasons, or because he had private speaking engagements — for which he billed schools and even charities up to $20,000 for the pleasure his company, even as an MP. When Trudeau became Liberal leader, his attendance at Question Period was still spotty

— just 39%, or about two days a week. And since becoming
Prime Minister, Trudeau has taken an unprecedented number of
vacations — ten in 2016, including a secret winter holiday at the
private island in the Bahamas, owned by a billionaire who just
happens to have huge contracts with the Canadian government
and is a registered lobbyist.

Trump has gorgeous getaways, too — luxury hotels that
bear his name around the world. But he built them, bought them
or licensed them. Trump flies in private jets — that he paid for.
Trudeau schmoozed and grifted his way into hotels on private
islands, and the private planes used to get there. Taking a private
island vacation worth $100,000 shows greed; hiring not one, but
two family nannies shows pettiness and entitlement.

Both men live large, but there's a difference: one took a half
million dollars from his father and turned it into billions; the other
took millions from his father and became a less-industrious version
of Paris Hilton.

There's a difference in work ethic, too. Trump had to fight
every step of the way for his presidency — against 16 other
Republican competitors for the party's nomination, including Jeb
Bush, the anointed candidate who raised and spent $130 million
from the party establishment; against Hillary Clinton's $1.2 billion
campaign; and against the entire media party, including, much of
the time, Fox News. Trump set a torrid pace, up to five stadium
rallies a day. It was a stunning work ethic for anyone half his age,
and he's kept that pace even after the election.

Trudeau, by contrast, had the Liberal Party leadership
practically handed to him. He did criss-cross the country, but

unlike Trump, who was running against prominent senators and governors, Trudeau was up against a handful of MPs and low-profile party activists with modest funding and no media support. Everyone agreed: it was Trudeau's destiny. His path to power was the same as what Jeb Bush's was supposed to to be.

Trump had celebrity status, and as long as he was considered a long shot, the media enjoyed the theatre of his campaign. But that turned to media fury once he won the nomination. And even after his election, the media's hostility reached new depths.

With Trudeau, the opposite happened: his media honeymoon lasted more than a year — something he helped ensure by massively increasing the government grant to the CBC state broadcaster.

Trudeau has always been the ultimate insider. Trump was the outsider — the risk taker, the street fighter who took on the establishment, sometimes successfully, sometimes not.

Both men have family foundations. Trump and his children have raised millions of dollars for charity. Trump himself has since shut down his foundation, to avoid the perception of conflicts of interest. The Trudeau Foundation has charitable status, but it doesn't give money to veterans or hospitals, like Trump's did. It's basically a private political operation, funding activists who just happen to support the Liberal Party's campaign platform. And, like Hillary Clinton's family foundation, its donations, especially from foreign lobbyists, have skyrocketed since Trudeau became party leader and then Prime Minister. Trudeau himself has grudgingly left the board of the foundation, but his brother remains on it. Business has never been better — including donations from a Chinese billionaires.

So, can either of these fortunate men claim to be for the working man?

The answer probably doesn't depend on the size of each leader's bank account, but rather his attitude and his actions.

Take the ritziest get-together in the world: the World Economic Forum, held each year in Davos, Switzerland. It's like a TED Talk, but for millionaires and billionaires. It's attended by politicians, wealthy businessmen and a few of the most politically annoying rock stars and actors, like Leonardo DiCaprio, Bono and will.i.am. It's like the Cannes Film Festival, but for ugly people. As Chrystia Freeland, Trudeau's new foreign minister, says, being invited to Davos "marks an aspiring plutocrat's arrival on the international scene."

It costs about $50,000 for a ticket — but you can only buy a ticket if you're a dues-paying member — and that can cost your company up to $500,000.

And that's the place Trudeau chose for his splashy international debut.

It wasn't his first foreign trip as Prime Minister — that was a G20 meeting in Turkey, which was followed by a whistle-stop tour through Europe, to visit the Queen, and then the Paris global warming conference. But his grand visit to the Davos festival was like a debutante's coming out party — accompanied by a massive entourage of Canadian journalists, there to photograph everything from Trudeau's socks, to his selfies with Kevin Spacey.

These were Trudeau's kind of people — senior executives from Facebook and Google, governors of half a dozen central banks, European Union big shots. And a thousand hangers-on who dropped six figures to be there.

There may have been some business done at Davos; certainly the companies that pay to hobnob think so. But their big payoff is to button-hole a world leader at a cocktail party — it's basically a frenzy for lobbyists. It's a private organization, not affiliated with any government. It passes no laws and makes not treaties.

Trudeau used it as a chance to talk about how feminist he was on an Oprah-style panel. That's Trudeau's style: that same week, key NATO allies were meeting to talk about their strategy to combat ISIS, and Trudeau wasn't invited. They probably wouldn't have had a session on feminism, anyway.

Every Canadian and American head of government puts some thought into his first major international tour. For Barack Obama, his keystone foreign policy speech was in Cairo, Egypt — which turned into the starting pistol for the Arab Spring. For Stephen Harper, it was a surprise trip to visit the Canadian Armed Forces in Afghanistan. Trump didn't go anywhere — he sat at home in Trump Tower and worked the phones, calling major American manufacturers, twisting their arms and bullying them on Twitter until they agreed to bring factory jobs back to America. Not only did he not go to Davos, he ordered no one from his team to go, either.

But the newly elected Trudeau chose to hobnob with billionaires at a Swiss ski resort. And when he wasn't talking himself up, he was talking down blue-collar workers in Canada. "My predecessor wanted you to know Canada for its resources," Trudeau said. "I want you to know Canadians for our resourcefulness." Facebook's executives must have smiled, but Facebook only employs 15,000 people worldwide, and only a sliver of that in Canada. Canada's resource industries employ 900,000 people directly. But they're not the cool kids drinking champagne in Switzerland.

Trump doesn't lack celebrity friends; he was the star of a top-rated TV show and he owned three different beauty pageants. But he's a blue-collar billionaire, if that's possible — the kind of guy who tweets a picture of himself eating McDonald's from his private jet.

But it wasn't just for show; Trump spent most of his time campaigning in places that the Davos set would call "flyover country" — industrial states in the Midwest that had been in decline, as mines and factories were shut down and often relocated to places like Mexico or Asia. Hillary Clinton took those states for granted: after she was nominated as the Democratic candidate, she didn't once campaign in the state of Wisconsin; Trump went there six times, including just two days before the election.

When Trump wears a hard hat with a suit, it looks a bit funny; but it's the suit that looks out of place, not the hard hat — everyone knows him as a builder and that's what builders wear on the job site. At Trump rallies, he didn't promise people entitlement programs. He promised them work, hard work — work in factories, work building a wall. He was a man wearing a suit that cost more than most people's mortgage payments. But he was cheering on coal miners and automakers. Even Michael Moore, the self-styled prophet of the abandoned blue-collar worker, couldn't help but be impressed. In a jam-packed theatre, in the middle of the election, Moore explained why, as an ardent Democrat, he had a grudging respect for the Republican:

"Donald Trump came to the Detroit Economic Club and stood there in front of Ford Motor executives and said, 'If you close these factories as you're planning to do in Detroit and build them in Mexico, I'm going to put a 35 percent tariff on those cars when you send them back and nobody's going to buy them.' It was an amazing thing to see. No politician, Republican or Democrat, had ever said anything like that to these executives, and it was music to the ears of people in Michigan and Ohio and Pennsylvania and Wisconsin — the 'Brexit states'."

An extended video clip of that speech went viral and Trump himself tweeted it to his followers. What was Hillary Clinton's rebuttal? Nothing, actually — she assumed she had the Midwest in the bag. She wouldn't be caught dead campaigning with hard hats — her preferred campaign surrogates were feminist social justice warriors like Lena Dunham and Beyoncé. They surely went down well at Clinton's Brooklyn campaign headquarters, but it didn't do much for middle-aged steelworkers in Pennsylvania.

Trudeau was cooler than Hillary Clinton. Her lame attempts at mastering social media sounded about as authentic as a 30-year-old narc going undercover at a high school. Trudeau connected with the 18-to-24-year-old set — namely students, or millennials still likely to be supported by their parents. But like Clinton, Trudeau was tone deaf towards working men, especially in manufacturing, especially those about to be squeezed by virtue-signalling regulations, like carbon taxes.

Even when Trudeau tries to be grassrootsy — when he makes a show of taking off his jacket and rolling up his sleeves — he still can't help the snobbery from slipping out. After his secret vacation on the billionaire's private island, Trudeau hastily arranged a cross-Canada tour to self-consciously "reconnect" with the middle class. But at a town hall meeting in Peterborough, Ontario, he absentmindedly reached for a talking point about the environment, and out came a threat: "We can't shut down the oilsands tomorrow. We need to phase them out. We need to manage the transition off of our dependence on fossil fuels."

Phase out an industry? Phase out the city of Fort McMurray, Alberta, phase out a hundred thousand direct jobs and a hundred thousand more that support them?

Kill real jobs — for a talking point?

It was the casualness of the statement that was so shocking: he didn't know he had stepped in it when he did; he didn't understand what the fuss was about; and his staff reacted angrily when that throwaway line made the news. Surely he'd heard that line a dozen times before from Gerald Butts, his principal advisor and former anti-oil lobbyist; surely he'd said it a dozen times himself — maybe not in public, but at least with his staff. Obviously no one had questioned him about it.

Like Obama's senior staff and cabinet, Trudeau doesn't have any real business leaders in his inner circle. There are scholars, activists, lawyers and career politicians. No capitalists, but no proletariat, either — these people are from a different social class; one that holds the other two in contempt. Like Obama, Trudeau has no one near him who is a doer or a maker, no one who spent years on a factory floor, or in a mine. Like Obama, Trudeau sees a business and thinks, "you didn't build that." Butts' own father had been a coal miner. But Butts himself couldn't be more different. He has two degrees in English Literature and made it part way through his PhD before he left for a life in politics. Phasing out jobs is something neither a coal miner nor a coal mine owner would want. It takes a special kind of snob to want that.

❖

It's hard to unlearn snobbery, especially so late in life. Trudeau had lived a life of wealth without work for a long time, and had surrounded himself with flatterers and sycophants. How many Alberta oil workers would a Montreal playboy have really ever met? To Trudeau, progressive politics has always meant other people tightening their belts, while he lived the trust-fund lifestyle. Ten years ago, the *Montreal Gazette* reported: "'We've never been willing to take the hit that is required, to give up quality of life,' said Trudeau, who blamed the 'wealthy' with their big cars and houses for using more than their proportionate share of our resources. Claiming he had more questions than answers, Trudeau said everyone has to think about what they're eating, where they're living and how they're getting around. 'Each and every one of us has a responsibility to think about the choices we make as consumers'."

That's just pious enough to get through a cocktail party in Montreal or Toronto; it hints at self-sacrifice, but doesn't actually call for any. It's odd to hear a criticism of fancy cars from the owner of a 1959 Mercedes Benz 300 SEL roadster, worth more than a million dollars. Is it a lack of self-awareness? Is it a giant joke — a sort of performance art, where Trudeau sees what he can get away with? Or is it his father's signature arrogance — the certain belief that he and his friends were philosopher kings; that they were above the grubby people, and if the ruling elite needed a few indulgences from time to time, that's the least the ungrateful masses could give them.

NINE

POCAHONTAS AND THE RAVEN TATTOO

There are real differences between Justin Trudeau and Donald Trump on substantive matters — taxes and the size of government, global warming and responses to it, the role of the military and the United Nations, trade deals and immigration. That's enough to keep the Canadian embassy in Washington working through the night for the next four years. But as large as any of those substantive differences are, the contrast in personal style between Trump and Trudeau is even bigger, and is more likely to become a flashpoint.

There are a hundred examples, but Trump's very New York practice of giving people nicknames is a good one — Crooked Hillary, Little Marco Rubio, Lyin' Ted Cruz. They seem to stick, because there's often a grain of truth to them, and they're funny. It's almost certain that Trudeau will end up with one.

But Trump got in trouble for one nickname he gave — or at least he was supposed to get in trouble for it. And how Trump handled that trouble is something Trudeau and his staff need to think about.

Trump just loves calling a far-left Senator from Massachusetts, Elizabeth Warren, "Pocahontas."

Warren is white — so white, she's pink. But when she was teaching at Harvard University, she claimed to be Native American. Except she's not — it was an affirmative action scam, a sure-fire way to be hired and promoted at a liberal institution. Some liberal spin-doctors claim she's $1/32^{nd}$ Cherokee, but there's no proof of that. The best Warren herself can muster is that she once heard her Aunt Bea tell her that her grandfather "had high cheekbones like all of the Indians do." Seriously.

Not everyone would be willing to run with that. Some would call it a bald-faced lie. But in today's politically correct world, where jobs and privileges and sometimes even legal rights are based on race or sex, it's surely a temptation. And anyone else who is shoved aside or passed over for an affirmative-action hire — typically boring "old white men" — well, they just learn to be quiet, lest they be called a bigot for objecting.

It's been going on for a while that way, from university faculties to fire departments: don't criticize affirmative action, or you'll be branded a racist or a sexist. But that's Trump's innovation: he just doesn't care.

Trump didn't start the fight with Warren — if you look at it carefully, he rarely does. But when someone starts taking pot-shots at him, he shoots back in a barrage of proverbial gunfire. Trump has called her "Pocahontas" nine times on Twitter, but that doesn't come close to capturing his love affair with the nickname — he went on extended riffs about it at campaign rallies. It got to the point where he wouldn't even use her real name; he'd just say, "Pocahontas," and people would know who he meant.

It was devastating — not just to Warren's reputation, but to the whole system. It proved one of Trump's major themes: that the system is rigged by insiders, who claim to be morally superior, but who have just written the rules for their own benefit.

Needless to say, the official people — the media, other politicians — were apoplectic. They demanded he apologize. And this is the part Trudeau's team should study: the moment when an Aboriginal activist, on live TV, called Trump offensive.

It was at a press conference in North Dakota. Trump was asked about Warren's attacks on him, and off he went. "Who, Pocahontas? Pocahontas?" he asked. Then, a Calgary-based Aboriginal journalist, Nicole Robertson, started heckling Trump: "Is that offensive? Very offensive, sorry." It was the kind of moment that makes journalistic careers — an Aboriginal woman speaking truth to power, saying what no one else would, calling Trump offensive. He was doomed — a young Aboriginal woman, versus a blustery old white guy? We know how that plays out.

Except it didn't. Trump didn't follow the script as he was supposed to — he didn't immediately apologize for causing "offence." He didn't ignore Robertson. He started sparring with her. "Is it offensive? You tell me. Oh, really, I'm sorry about that." And then he kept on going, immediately saying "Pocahontas" again. "I think she's as native American as I am," he said.

Was it offensive? Could be — being offended is subjective. Anyone could find anything offensive. Is it racist? It's an allusion to race — but only to mock a white liberal who is taking advantage of racial quotas for her own benefit. If Trump had mocked an Aboriginal woman as "Pocahontas," it could have come across differently. But he was doing the opposite — showing just how white Warren was, and how much of a scammer she was. But Nicole Robertson gave Trump one more thing: the chance to show how unafraid he was of gotcha-style politically correct journalism.

How many conservatives, when accused of racism, would immediately backpedal and apologize? How many would be flustered and knocked off course? How many would let themselves be defined that way? Every other one — just like Mitt Romney was in 2012 and John McCain was in 2008, and every other conservative loser in the U.S. and Canada, too. That's what Justin Trudeau and his media couriers in Canada call "Sunny Ways" — it really means that no one is allowed to say mean things about the left or its sacred cows. Trump wasn't even challenging the concept of racial quotas; he was pointing out the farce they have become if a white woman can profit from them.

And in that moment, he was an avatar for everyone in America who had ever been passed over because of race, or thought they were. That was Trump getting even for them — smacking back at someone who had taken their job. And not caving into the race-hucksters who enforce language correctness. There's nothing inherently wrong with saying "Pocahontas" — it's the name of a historic person. It's not a derogatory slur. Trump just weaponized it. But it was jarring and liberals hated it, and the word police arrived.

Trudeau's government is full of word police. It's not just a sign of how modern they are; it's a way of keeping outsiders out, and down. If you don't know their inside codes, you're not just uncool, you're probably a bigot. In Canada, the law governing reserves is called the Indian Act; the government department was changed to use the word "Aboriginal" instead; and Trudeau has changed the government's terminology to "Indigenous." If you don't use the right word, it's proof you're a racist. The Indian Act itself really is racist — it gives and takes away legal rights based on race; it was the template for South Africa's Apartheid laws. But to the Liberals, whether you say "Indian," "First Nations" or "Indigenous" is more important than actually solving the problem. Solving the problem is hard work that involves action; saying the right things is good for photo-ops and TED Talks.

Barack Obama was a master of language politics, too. He knew the power of calling people racist or sexist. And he knew the political importance of banning worlds from the official vocabulary — words like "Islamic terrorism" and "illegal immigrant." Even the name of the terrorist group, the Islamic State, was replaced by a meaningless Arabic nickname, "Daesh," in order to remove the constant reminder to listeners that the terrorist group is Muslim in nature.

It's in the little things. Trump would riff at length about how he loves to say "merry Christmas" in a world where people are told to say "seasons greetings." It's not a symbol of Trump's devout religiosity; it's a symbol of his rejection of the hectoring and scolding that fancy people use to keep everyone else in line.

So much of the Trudeau Liberal playbook is name-calling in its own way — the Liberals adopted Hillary Clinton's thesis that if you criticize a female politician, it's because you're misogynist. Anyone who wants to ban the Muslim burka in citizenship court

— which is the vast majority of Canadians, according to polls — is simply "Islamophobic." Trump was called everything from a sex criminal to Hitler during the campaign, and his popularity only rose.

Americans wouldn't vote for a criminal or a fascist. What the U.S. pundit class didn't realize is that by calling Trump those names, the media was also calling Trump supporters those names, and they had enough of it. The more extreme the demonization of Trump, the more people could relate to him — especially when the attacks came from Hollywood or media elites. The attacks made him stronger; when Hillary Clinton called Trump supporters a "basket of deplorables," Trump made it into a devastating ad showing her contempt for ordinary people.

So far, most of the world's leaders have been wise enough to notice this dynamic that Clinton seemed to miss. And if foreign leaders have disagreements with Trump, they're careful not to phrase them in personal attacks.

That's the bigger risk for Trudeau: if he thinks he's going to shame Trump, he won't just provoke a retaliation from the New York tough guy himself. He'll risk turning ordinary Americans against Canada, too.

TEN

THE ART OF THE DEAL

Theresa May, the British Prime Minister, is off to a rollicking start with Donald Trump. She set the tone by breaking with Barack Obama's approach to the United Nations and Israel. Trump did what he always does: he responded in kind, promising a very speedy negotiation of a U.S.-U.K. trade agreement, and pledging to make "Brexit" a success.

Trump is by nature a deal-maker; his most famous book is his 1987 combination autobiography and self-help book called *The Art of the Deal*. It's the best decoder ring to understanding what Trump says and does — even his penchant for making shocking and outrageous statements. Trump explains how he uses the media, how he makes outlandish offers and how he uses hyperbole. It may look chaotic or accidental, but it's all part of a strategy, or at least a mindset. It's hardball, it's rude and sometimes it might not even seem fair. But part of the value proposition that so many voters had was: he may fight unfair, but he's going to fight unfair for me. All the skills and tricks that made Trump great will now be deployed to making America great. That's something Hillary Clinton didn't get when she attacked Trump for his tax-avoidance strategies. She thought it made him look too clever and too selfish; to millions of voters, it surely made him look like just the kind of guy needed to give America a few wins, after being the world's chump for so long.

Take airplanes. At 6:52 a.m. on December 6, 2016, when most Americans were still sleeping, Trump tweeted two dozen words: "Boeing is building a brand new 747 Air Force One for future presidents, but costs are out of control, more than $4 billion. Cancel order!" Boeing stock plunged by $1 billion when the markets opened, and Boeing executives scrambled to save the deal, promising to meet Trump half way — all this, a month before he was even sworn in. It was re-tweeted more than 142,000 times by other people, startled by the audacity of it, but enjoying the feeling of Trump's boldness being used to promote their interests. The military-industrial complex is used to passing cost overruns on to taxpayers without any noisy objection from politicians. I mean, what could they do, cancel the order? Well, that's exactly what Trump threatened to do, and whether he was serious or not, it was enough to get shocked Boeing executives to get on the phone and beg.

That's how he managed to avoid being tagged an out-of-touch billionaire — he may be a billionaire, but he's the only one who's been thinking of the taxpayers' interests. Trump was so pleased with his negotiating approach, he rolled it out a week later, with another military supplier, Lockheed Martin, tweeting at 6:26 a.m.: "The F-35 program and cost is out of control. Billions of dollars can and will be saved on military (and other) purchases after January 20th." That must have got their attention, too — Lockheed-Martin's stock fell by $4 billion that day.

It's tough talk, it's bombastic, it might even be called unprofessional by fancy people. You just don't do that — you call up lobbyists and talk it out over steaks at some luxury restaurant in Washington, D.C., and maybe some political donations are very carefully mentioned in the background. Trump was showing that his style — the very style that all the delicate people were warning about — is exactly what was missing. In two tweets, he saved American taxpayers billions of dollars, and proved he was beholden to no one. Not bad for a few moments worth of work before breakfast.

Compare that to Justin Trudeau. He's currently involved in some negotiations with aircraft companies, too. But he's the anti-Trump — he's giving taxpayer money away to a company, for free, behind closed doors. Bombardier, Quebec's perennial corporate welfare bum, is begging for more handouts from Trudeau. And Trudeau's response is like reading Trump's *Art of the Deal* in reverse.

Trudeau had been negotiating with Bombardier for months — Bombardier lobbyists were regular visitors to Ottawa, but no deal was announced. Reuters news agency asked Trudeau what the hold-up was and if there was any chance the government would just walk away from the talks.

"I don't think there's any point at which you don't want to build greater opportunities in the Canadian economy... we're always open to looking at ways of strengthening and creating better jobs," he said. Trump knows you never appear more eager than the other guy; the "negotiation" in question here was a one-way gift, from taxpayers to Bombardier, a multi-billion-dollar company with billionaire owners and millionaire executives. They had no business leg to stand on — it wasn't a business deal, it was corporate welfare they were after. And they were hardly a sympathetic recipient of tax largess. But Trudeau let them know that he really wouldn't say no to them, when push came to shove. In fact, he took some time making their arguments for them. Bombardier, he said, "is exactly where the Canadian economy needs to continue to go." He went even further in an interview with Bloomberg News: he put a deadline on himself. "That is exactly what we are working on and we hope to have announcements to make before the budget."

Bombardier isn't the only aircraft negotiation Trudeau is involved with. Like the U.S., Canada is part of the F-35 fighter jet program, a status that had led to $1 billion in contracts for Canadian firms — Canada just spent another $36 million to stay part of the consortium. But Trudeau swore he would never buy F-35s — they are too closely associated with Stephen Harper, so that's all he needed to know. He's decided to buy Boeing Super Hornets as a stop-gap — yet he still expects Lockheed-Martin to give billions in contracts to Canadian companies. But after Trump made his cost-busting tweet, Trudeau reversed course, saying that Canada still will consider the F-35 — but not for sure, and the government won't decide for five years. Like Trudeau himself, his position on fighter jets is not exactly coherent or decisive.

Negotiating complex deals is not something that Trudeau, or anyone in his office or in his cabinet, have ever done. They just haven't. Gerald Butts, Trudeau's principal secretary, describes himself online as "an experienced executive" and "senior leader," and that's true. But his experience is in academia and environmental lobby groups — where billionaires donated the money and Butts spent it. His time working in the office of former Ontario premier Dalton McGuinty showed how disastrous Butts really is when it comes to complex systems and business negotiations: the Green Energy Act he championed was an operational disaster, but more than that, according to Ontario's auditor general, over the lifetime of the program, Ontario will spend $170 billion more than necessary on wind and solar power. That's the guy who will be helping Trudeau with the hard part of negotiating.

Canada's defence minister, Harjit Sajjan, is probably the closest thing Trudeau has to an executive in his cabinet — Sajjan commanded an army reserve regiment, and in Afghanistan, as well as in his role as a Vancouver police officer, he certainly made life or death decisions in real time. Those are useful skills, and will provide common ground when dealing with Trump's nominee for defence secretary, General James "Mad Dog" Mattis. But Sajjan isn't the decider on military missions; that's clearly Trudeau, as was shown in his very first phone call with Barack Obama. If Canada and the U.S. ever do decide to fight a military mission together, as Trump plans to do against ISIS, Sajjan will likely have an excellent rapport with his American counterpart, and effectively execute the plan. But it's agreeing to the plan in the first place that's the problem, and that's not something Sajjan controls.

Trudeau clearly needs a middleman — and not the Marxist English literature major, Gerald Butts. Canada's ambassador to Washington, David MacNaughton, made sense when he was

appointed in early 2016 — MacNaughton worked closely with
Butts in Dalton McGuinty's office, and he's a well-connected
lobbyist. He was the perfect go-between when the two principals
involved — Trudeau and Obama — were so friendly to begin with,
and MacNaughton was inoffensive enough to the Republican
Congress, too.

There is no real problem with MacNaughton himself — it's
just that with Trump, having someone who really clicks with
him is such a bonus. Trump said as much when he tweeted the
suggestion that the United Kingdom appoint his pal, former
U.K. Independence Party leader Nigel Farage, as its ambassador
to Washington. It was an outrageous request — tantamount to
asking to choose the other side's lawyer in court. But it showed
that Trump values personal relationships and he hates fussy
bureaucratic bores. Being boring is an important quality in a
diplomat, most of the time — any news is bad news and any
rash word is a possible international incident. But Trump enjoys
working with like-minded people, including those who share his
disruptive approach to the status quo. Should Trudeau find a new
Canadian ambassador, who's a better fit?

It's what Stephen Harper did. Harper appointed Michael
Wilson — a pro-business former finance minister under Brian
Mulroney — to be the bridge to George W. Bush's White House.
But when Barack Obama won in 2008, Harper made the strategic
choice to replace Wilson with Gary Doer, the sitting NDP premier
of Manitoba. Harper literally plucked him out of office to send him
to Washington, to better connect with Obama and the Democrat-
controlled Congress of the day. It was a brilliant decision, not
just given Doer's socialist credentials, but his Manitoba-friendly

personality, too. It wasn't about Harper's partisan interests, or his personal taste. It was about keeping a constructive relationship with a very different White House.

Could Trudeau do that, too?

Could he find a Canadian who was deeply loyal to Canada, but the kind of person who Trump would look forward to meeting, who would have the same worldview as Trump — being plain-spoken, with a bias towards action and real-life entrepreneurial experience?

Trump hasn't suggested such a person, as he did with Farage. But he does have Canadian friends — like Conrad Black, the former media tycoon who was one of Trump's biggest boosters in the Canadian press. Black wouldn't forget his first loyalty to Canada, but he shares Trump's grand vision. Black's last book is called *Rise to Greatness: The History of Canada*. That almost sounds like "Make Canada Great Again."

Or maybe a more radical choice, someone more like Trump himself — a builder, who could talk for hours with Trump about deals and construction and taxes, someone who has lived it, not just read about it in briefing notes. Toronto has plenty of tall towers with big personalities behind them. Maybe someone like Howard Sokolowski — a builder with more than 30,000 homes to his credit, including some very tall towers, who also made the Trump-like move of owning a CFL team for years. Sokolowski is married to Linda Frum, a Conservative senator. But like Harper's choice of Gary Doer, it's a symbol of good faith. And when it comes to negotiating, whether its trade deals, or military missions, it would be nice if Trudeau had one person on his team who had actually spent a life in business.

TRUDEAU'S CHOICE

Like most liberals around the world, Justin Trudeau is still in shock from Donald Trump's victory.

There were warning tremors — like the U.K. referendum on leaving the European Union. That wasn't supposed to happen: all the good and great people were against it. Everyone but the people, it seems.

Trump's win wasn't even supposed to be scientifically possible — pollsters said so, and they had the math to prove it. But it wasn't just a win, it was a blowout, with Midwestern states voting Republican for the first time in a generation.

Most liberal institutions still don't know what to do — the media is frothing, both in Canada and the U.S. Hollywood is threatening to go on strike. Even the United Nations is in a daze — delegates to their annual global warming convention were like zombies, going through the motions, knowing that none of it likely mattered any more.

Some hard-core liberal activists are already planning the

counter-revolution, led of course by George Soros. But things are likely going to keep getting worse for them, as Trump's right-wing cabinet takes office and starts to flex its muscles on everything from the EPA, to the UN, to ISIS.

And 2017 itself will bring more shocks, with elections in France, Germany and the Netherlands all trending towards conservative nationalism.

So what will Trudeau do? Will he stay loyal to his friends in the globalist left — the billionaires he hobnobbed with at Davos, the liberal activists who feted him in New York and Washington? It's tempting: from Chrystia Freeland to Gerald Butts, his entire inner circle holds the Democrats as not only role models, but friends. They want to disrupt and delegitimize Trump, and Trudeau obviously does, too. But how is that in Canada's interests?

Justin Trudeau and the Liberals have a choice to make: turn Canada into the leader of the opposition for the whole world, or serve Canada's interests carefully and constructively, and make the best of the next four years.

There are plenty of people who want to use Trudeau as a battering ram against Trump — the same way Pierre Trudeau was used by everyone from the Soviets to the Castro's to embarrass and undermine America and NATO during the Cold War. Trudeau the elder enjoyed the naughty celebrity status that came from flirting with the enemy. Justin Trudeau, and his brother Alexandre, clearly have that same instincts, with their ostentatious affections for Iran, China and Cuba today. One difference is, Donald Trump is less likely to bite his tongue than past U.S. presidents. And he's on the warpath against U.S. companies building things in foreign countries and then importing them back to America for sale.

There's a word for a place that does that: Ontario.

The Cold War let Pierre Trudeau play both sides — he'd flirt with the Soviets, hinting that if the U.S. didn't like what he was doing, he'd flirt with them more. But today, Russia is eager to reconcile with Trump and it's Canada's foreign minister, Chrystia Freeland who is banned from even travelling to Russia. It's different in a world with just one hyperpower — you can't play one side off against the other anymore.

The world's leftists are trying to get Trudeau to be their champion now. Obama roped Trudeau into his last-gasp ban on Arctic drilling. Obama's VP, Joe Biden, came to Ottawa after the U.S. election and practically asked Trudeau to oppose the next president: "The world is going to spend a lot of time looking to you Mr. Prime Minister as we see more and more challenges to the liberal international order than any time since the end of World War Two," he said. "You and Angela Merkel."

It was strange for Trudeau to host Biden so lavishly, so close to Trump's ascent. It was stranger still that Biden used the occasion to call for opposition to his own country. But that's got to be intoxicating for any Canadian to hear, especially one with a bit of a messiah complex, like Trudeau. Not only can Trudeau save Canada from Harper, he can save the world from Trump.

The media sure hope so. The *Economist* magazine praised Trudeau as the last, best hope of the liberal west:

"Canada's openness is not new, but it is suddenly getting global attention. It is a happy contrast to what is happening in other rich countries, where anger about immigration helped bring about Britain's vote for Brexit, Donald Trump's nomination and the rise of populist parties across Europe. And it has an appealing new face: Justin Trudeau celebrates his first anniversary as Prime Minister on November 4th."

They helpfully compiled a list of quotes from the global super elite, who praised Trudeau, mainly for being the anti-Trump: to European and American liberals, he is a champion of embattled values and his country a haven with many charms. "The world needs more Canada," said Bono, the activist and lead singer of U2, in September. When in Ottawa recently, the IMF's chief, Christine Lagarde, said she hoped Canada's pump-priming economic policies would "go viral." Trump's Super Tuesday victories saw Google searches for "How to move to Canada" surge south of the border.

Sure they did. But no celebrities who publicly swear to leave America actually do leave; they didn't after George W. Bush won, either. Shortly after that article was published, Christine Lagarde was found guilty of abuse of power, involving a half-billion dollar scandal. And U2, well, they're just being U2. Normal people don't care what the elites think anymore; if they did, Beyonce and Katy Perry would be performing at the inauguration, not military marching bands.

It's so tempting — Trudeau's vanity, plus Trudeau's loyalty, plus the praise of the world's remaining elites. All Justin Trudeau has to do is say what they say and help bring Donald Trump down a peg. That's what they really want. U2 doesn't care about Canada and neither does Christine Lagarde. They just want someone else to dash themselves against the rock of Donald Trump, like the last hundred liberals to do so.

It's a good project for a gonzo filmmaker like Michael Moore, but not such a good idea for the Prime Minister of a neighbouring country.

Justin Trudeau must stand up for Canadian interests; and if that means he needs to disagree with U.S. policy, he must do so. Despite all of our trade and military alliances with the United States, Canada is still an independent country. But that's not what Trudeau's done so far — he's scolded and taunted and provoked. Lucky for him, Trump has been too busy with China and Mexico to notice. That will change, and before it does, Trudeau had better resign himself to the fact that the liberal utopia he and his team had been dreaming about will never be built.

The Justin Trudeau Era is over. It's the Age of Trump now. The two men will never be friends, but for the sake of our two countries, they need to be partners.

ABOUT THE REBEL.MEDIA

TheRebel.media is a leading independent source of news, opinion and activism. Launched by Ezra Levant and a group of dedicated Rebels after The Sun News Network shutdown. The Rebel is essential for anyone looking for "the other side of the story" in Conservative news in Canada and across the world.

www.therebel.media

CPSIA information can be obtained
at www.ICGtesting.com
Printed in the USA
LVOW07s1543300917
550687LV00018B/345/P

9 781542 526203